Itsy Bitsy Yoga

for Toddlers and Preschoolers

Itsy Bitsy Yoga®

for Toddlers and Preschoolers

● ● ●

8-Minute Routines to Help Your Child
Grow Smarter, Be Happier, and Behave Better

Helen Garabedian

Da Capo

LIFE
LONG

A Member of the Perseus Books Group

DESIGN BY JANE RAESE
Set in 12-point New Baskerville

Cataloging-in-Publication Data for this book is available from the Library of Congress.

First Da Capo Press edition 2008
ISBN-10 1-60094-008-0
ISBN-13 978-1-60094-008-8

Published by Da Capo Press
A Member of the Perseus Books Group
www.dacapopress.com

Note: The information in this book is true and complete to the best of our knowledge. This book is intended only as an informative guide for those wishing to know more about health issues. In no way is this book intended to replace, countermand, or conflict with the advice given to you by your own physician. The ultimate decision concerning care should be made between you and your doctor. We strongly recommend you follow his or her advice. Information in this book is general and is offered with no guarantees on the part of the authors or Da Capo Press. The authors and publisher disclaim all liability in connection with the use of this book.

Da Capo Press books are available at special discounts for bulk purchases in the United States by corporations, institutions, and other organizations. For more information, please contact the Special Markets Department at the Perseus Books Group, 2300 Chestnut Street, Suite 200, Philadelphia, PA 19103, or call (800) 255-1514, or e-mail special.markets@ perseusbooks.com.

LSC-C
20 19 18 17 16 15 14 13 12 11

This book is dedicated to Andrew Garabedian,
my toddler who continuously inspires and delights me!
And also to my family, friends, and students,
who help me share my purpose, passion, and creation
of Itsy Bitsy Yoga with the world!

And with profound thanks to the lyrics from the folk song,
"This Little Light of Mine."

This little light of mine,
I'm gonna let it shine.
This little light of mine,
I'm gonna let it shine.
This little light of mine,
I'm gonna let it shine.
Let it shine,
Let it shine,
Let it shine.

Contents

● ● ●

Introduction

· · ·

If you have a young child, you'll love what this book has to offer you. *Itsy Bitsy Yoga for Toddlers and Preschoolers* is a unique blend of yoga-based postures and games, developmental movement exercises, and playful rhymes I have created to increase parent-child bonding and promote a healthy lifestyle for families with young children. In this book, you will find over fifty easy-to-learn and practical poses that can benefit children as early as eighteen months up to five years old. In just minutes, you will learn ways to practice yoga and make your days easier—from calming your toddler as you rinse the shampoo out of her hair to helping her get dressed with ease. When you and your child have more time, you can practice one or more of the eight-minute yoga routines that build strength, flexibility, and motor skills.

Why I Began Teaching *Itsy Bitsy Yoga*

I am grateful for this opportunity to share my passion for yoga and healthy family living with you. Some of my fondest childhood memories are of practicing yoga with my mom and learning how to meditate from my dad. Now that I am a mother of a toddler, I love sharing yoga with my son. My passion for and education in early childhood development, yoga, and family life led me to create the *Itsy Bitsy*

Yoga® program in 1999. Today, *Itsy Bitsy Yoga* classes are taught in over a dozen countries around the world by Certified Facilitators who have trained with me personally. Along the way, I have presented lectures at the largest early childhood conferences in the country, written books and articles, and produced DVDs so that *Itsy Bitsy Yoga* for babies, toddlers, and preschoolers can be accessible to parents everywhere.

In teaching yoga to thousands of families, I have seen firsthand the benefits of yoga for toddlers, which include:

- Fewer tantrums
- Better sleep
- Improved digestion
- Higher self-esteem
- Increased listening skills
- Better self-expression
- Improved gross and fine motor development
- Easier relaxation
- A healthy and physically fit lifestyle

I am passionate about my life's work because of these benefits. I also want parents everywhere to understand the importance of parent-child bonding; how vital gross and fine motor development is to school readiness; and how health and exercise habits we help our toddlers develop now affect our children throughout their lives.

In this book, I will teach you more than fifty yoga poses and games to encourage the physical, social, emotional, and cognitive development of your toddlers and preschoolers. As an Infant and Early Childhood Developmental Movement Specialist who has trained with some of the best pediatricians and pediatric physical therapists in the country, I am aware of the many gross and fine motor skills a child needs before entering kindergarten. Some of the poses in this book are adapted from traditional yoga; others I have created to help each participant develop a strong and confident body, mind, and spirit.

Fitness for Life

Over the past twenty years, obesity has tripled among adolescents and doubled among children in the United States. The rapid increase in obesity is due to a decrease in physical activity and an increase in sedentary activities such as watching television, sitting at a computer, and playing video games. Obesity is more than being overweight or fat; it comes with an onslaught of problems, such as diabetes, cardio-vascular disease, psychological and emotional problems, sleep distur-bances, orthopedic problems, and more colds. The way to prevent and treat obesity is to get physically active early in life when lifelong habits are forming. Researchers believe that active toddlers and preschoolers will grow into active children, who then become active teens who remain active throughout adulthood.

My mantra is "A Fit Baby = A Fit Toddler = A Fit Preschooler = A Fit School-Aged Child = A Fit Teen = A Fit Adult." Early in life, parents influence a child's health habits, and these early health habits can last a lifetime. As parents and caregivers, we need to emphasize the importance of healthy eating habits and work to increase the amount of structured physical activities our young children participate in each day.

In 2002, the National Association for Sports and Physical Educa-tion (NASPE) set the first-ever physical guidelines for infants and tod-dlers. NASPE recommends the following daily physical activity guidelines for toddlers:

- Thirty minutes of accumulated structured physical activity daily
- Sixty minutes to several hours of unstructured physical activity daily
- No more than sixty minutes of sedentary behavior at a time when awake

With *Itsy Bitsy Yoga*, you help your family meet these NASPE guide-lines. The routines in this book can provide you and your young children with the structured physical activities that you can enjoy in the comfort of your home. *Itsy Bitsy Yoga* can help you cultivate a healthier, harmonious, and caring family.

Who Can Benefit from This Book?

Itsy Bitsy Yoga delights parents, grandparents, aunts, uncles, pediatric medical professionals, preschool teachers, and daycare center workers with its healthy, noncompetitive approach to physical fitness and early childhood development. Toddlers and preschoolers love *Itsy Bitsy Yoga* so much that parents often catch their little ones practicing *Itsy Bitsy Yoga* poses on their own and with their toys!

This book provides fun, age-appropriate exercises and relaxation skills especially created for almost two- through five-year-old children to enjoy with a parent or caregiver. You can choose to learn *Itsy Bitsy Yoga* at home with this book, in *Tykes Itsy Bitsy Yoga* classes taught by trained and Certified *Itsy Bitsy Yoga* Facilitators, or through my multimedia products. To learn more, visit our Web site at itsybitsyyoga.com.

Is My Toddler Too Young to Start Yoga?

No one is ever too young (or too old) to start the practice of yoga. Parents and caregivers are invited to start practicing the postures in this book with children as young as eighteen months and as old as five years. If you have a baby or younger tot in your home, you may want to read my first book, *Itsy Bitsy Yoga: Poses to Help Your Baby Sleep Longer, Digest Better and Grow Stronger* (Simon & Schuster, 2004). It provides over seventy poses designed for children younger than twenty-one months.

Do I Get to Do Yoga Too?

Yes! The more yoga you do, the more yoga your toddler will do too. Toddlers and preschoolers learn yoga poses best by watching someone else demonstrate the yoga pose first. That someone is you! *Itsy Bitsy Yoga* for toddlers and preschoolers enables you to practice yoga and adds exercise into your day.

No Yoga Experience Needed

No experience is necessary to share yoga with your toddler or preschooler. *Itsy Bitsy Yoga* can help anyone—with or without yoga experience—move, stretch, and play with their children.

chapter 1
How Yoga Can Help You and Your Child

● ● ●

For the toddler or preschooler participant, *Itsy Bitsy Yoga* can help tame tantrums, encourage better sleep, improve digestion, develop self-esteem, increase listening skills, cultivate self-expression, promote gross and fine motor development, provide relaxation techniques, and develop a healthy and physically fit lifestyle. Toddlers and preschoolers who have practiced *Itsy Bitsy Yoga* appear to have greater physical abilities and are better behaved compared to other children. Parents attribute these benefits to yoga.

Parents who practice *Itsy Bitsy Yoga* with their child notice a deeper parent-child bond, happier days, more restful nights, and a greater confidence in their parenting skills, which leads to less stress and anxiety. Since adults are invited to do each pose with their child, this book helps you get additional exercise. For parents with more than one child, *Itsy Bitsy Yoga* is also a special way to spend quality one-on-one time while enjoying your toddler or preschooler. By incorporating yoga into your young child's day, I am confident you will begin to notice the benefits I will discuss throughout this chapter.

Fewer Tantrums

Cheryl, the mother of two-year-old Noah, was in the middle of her husband's workplace with her toddler when he broke out into a tantrum. Cheryl was so embarrassed! "My husband had only been with this company for a few months, and this was our first visit to his office," she recalls. Many employees were nearby and at first Cheryl didn't know what to do. But then she remembered a tip I had shared with her in class earlier that week. She scooped up her flailing and fussy toddler and went into an empty cubicle. Cheryl sat on the office chair, held Noah on her lap, and began to spin round and round. Cheryl was following my On the Go with Helen component for Silly Spins (page 115), a modification of the pose. Noah's tantrum quickly transformed into laughter—luckily, just as her husband's boss walked by. Later that night, Cheryl's husband told her his boss said, "Wow, your wife really knows how to calm your son!"

Yoga is calming for adults and its effects are the same on young children. I find my more energetic poses can calm toddlers during a tantrum. Parents tell me that on the days they and their children do yoga, their children fuss less and there are no tantrums!

When you follow the poses in this book precisely, especially those in the Tantrum Taming Yoga routine (page 111) and Run, Rock n' Roll Yoga routine (page 71), you may notice that tantrums and fussy outbreaks are a thing of the past! When yoga helps tame your toddler, you'll enjoy your time with your toddler more and be less stressed.

Better and Longer Sleep

One of the main reasons why kids sleep more soundly and longer after yoga is that yoga provides a healthy dose of physical exercise. Yoga engages muscles and then releases them, leaving a toddler feeling relaxed and content. Not only will this improve your child's sleep, your toddler will be better behaved and happier if he or she is getting enough sleep. The two routines to help your young child ease into quiet time and sleep better are Quiet Time Yoga (page 165) and Blissful Bedtime Yoga (page 185).

The Quiet Time Yoga routine is a great pre-nap activity. And if your toddler is weaning herself from naps, you'll absolutely love the benefits of a midday Quiet Time Yoga practice.

The Blissful Bedtime Yoga routine is an affectionate, empowering, and fun way to end the day. Before bed, Gabrielle, mother of almost three-year-old Brooke, loves to share the "Special You" song (page 200) with her daughter. They were introduced to the song when Brooke, then three months old, was in my *Baby Itsy Bitsy Yoga* class. The "Special You" song has become a staple of their bedtime routine ever since. Gabrielle recently told me that Brooke now enjoys singing the "Special You" song to her mommy and daddy too! So sweet!

Improved Digestion

For years, yoga has helped its adult practitioners digest by gently strengthening and massaging the intestines through movement and body positioning. You'll find a number of yoga poses in this book that can help your young child release abdominal gas and constipation. Here's a list of a few of my favorite poses for digestive relief:

- Child (page 43)
- Kissy Knee (page 190)
- Cat (page 37)
- Cow (page 39)
- Ball (page 153)
- Lil' Yogi (page 192)

Higher Self-Esteem

Itsy Bitsy Yoga empowers toddlers and preschoolers through words, actions, and yoga. When a new session begins, I notice that some children enter with a defeatist attitude. I am shocked to see a toddler feel like he can not do such and such. With *Itsy Bitsy Yoga*, you teach your child about all the things he can do! The program is developmentally centered so that toddlers can learn and achieve mentally, physically, and emotionally. When a preschooler starts to show mastery and a readiness for more, I love to challenge him or her with the Yogi Wogi Says technique you will find throughout this book.

It is also important to remember that if your young child's expression of a yoga pose looks unrefined, please practice the yogic principles of acceptance and nonjudgment. Every message we send to a young child about movement and their bodies should be positive and encouraging. The undistracted, one-on-one time yoga offers lets your child know that she is important and worthy of your attention. The attention you pay to your toddler is like making a deposit into the bank of good behavior and long-lasting self-esteem!

Better Listening Skills

Many parents are pleasantly surprised to see how well their young children listen to my directions during class. In addition to listening, toddlers and preschoolers eagerly follow and act upon my directions! Young children listen to me and Certified *Itsy Bitsy Yoga* Facilitators because we are highly skilled in speaking in a way that toddlers can understand. During the Say n' Play section of each pose in this book, I will teach you how to speak with your toddler in a way that is easy for him or her to understand. This will help your toddler listen to and act upon your directions. Once you begin to understand how simple, repetitive statements best suit your toddler's ears, you'll enjoy a toddler who is more willing to listen to and respond to your requests.

Increased Self-Expression

A few of the poses in this book were created by toddlers and pre-schoolers in my classes. For instance, Jumping Tree (page 122) was invented by three-and-a-half-year-old Jenna. She came to class one day and said, "Look what I can do!" I loved how her pose playfully cultivated development, so the Jumping Tree pose was born. For Jenna, *Itsy Bitsy Yoga* served as an impetus to her creativity and self-expression. On the other hand, not every pose a young child makes up is a keeper. Typically when a young child discovers a new way to move through a pose, I smile and offer praise. That's what young children truly want and need—to feel connected with their bodies and creativity!

Reduced Stress

Studies show that children today encounter 25 percent more stress than their grandparents did as children. As parents, we need to realize the importance of teaching relaxation techniques to our young children. It is never too early to offer your children tools to release the stressors of toddlerhood and preschool. Yoga triggers endorphins—the body's natural "feel good" hormones—which combat stress and help children be prepared to learn. Children who are constantly in stressful situations without stress-relieving tools, such as yoga and exercise, have difficulty learning and remaining focused.

Fiona, a mother of two, once shared with me how she coached her toddler to endure some uncomfortable medical situations by using the yoga poses and breathing techniques they learned in *Itsy Bitsy Yoga.*

Parenting a two- to five-year-old child can certainly be stressful, and *Itsy Bitsy Yoga* will help alleviate some of that stress. I notice that when parents have a deeper connection with their child and also know how to calm their child, they experience less stress than those who don't.

Some of my favorite stress-relieving activities are Lion's Breath (page 120), In and Out (page 170), Count n' Breathe (page 55), and Burrito (page 87).

Improved Gross and Fine Motor Development

Your child's ability to succeed in school depends largely on his or her gross and fine motor skills. All the poses that your toddler or preschooler practices while on all fours (mostly in the Wake n' Stretch Yoga routine) will boost the fine motor skills needed for buttoning clothes, zippering jackets, and holding crayons. Poses that provide young children with opportunities to bear weight on their forearms, such as Cobra (page 82) and Wanna Iguana (page 85), help strengthen the muscles used in handwriting. Poses such as I Like … (page 197), Rag Doll (page 106), and My Planet (page 172) can help young ones focus and recenter their energy. Some of my playful movement rhymes, such as Itsy Bitsy Yogi (page 129), can boost hand-eye coordination. Many other poses teach breathing and relaxation skills so your child will be better equipped to release stress. In just a few minutes a day, you can give your young child a foundation for success in school and, most importantly, a loving family life.

A Healthy, Physically Fit Lifestyle

Toddlers and preschoolers need ample time each day to move, explore, and test the capabilities of their rapidly developing bodies and minds. Without meeting the National Association of Sports and Physical Education minimum requirement of thirty minutes of structured physical activity each day, a toddler's future health and exercise habits can be jeopardized. When you devote time to positively affect your toddler's development with yoga, you are helping him or her build a collection of gross and fine motor skills that will become vital in school readiness and sports.

Parents set a toddler's foundation for a physically active childhood and beyond. Confined and sedentary toddlers grow into sedentary children. *Itsy Bitsy Yoga* is designed in accordance with the physical activity guidelines set forth by the National Association for Sport and Physical Education for children from birth to five years old. This exercise program will also help you relieve tension and stress and allow you to focus more fully on your child. Yoga can easily become one of the structured physical activities that you and your toddler can enjoy together.

Strengthened Bonds between Parent and Child

Yoga means to unite. During *Itsy Bitsy Yoga,* parents are further united with their young children. *Itsy Bitsy Yoga* gives you a natural, toy-free way to play with your toddler or preschooler. This program will help you make your child feel special in your presence. During yoga, the parent and young child are better able to step away from any distractions and focus solely on learning about each other. You and your toddler will bond in yoga through the senses, singing, moving, learning, and breathing.

Sarah has two children, a two-year-old boy and an eight-month-old baby girl. She loves having two children so close in age but feels guilty about the lack of quality one-on-one time. Sarah is concerned that she may have spread herself too thin. After juggling her schedule and arranging for her mother-in-law to babysit, Sarah comes to *Itsy Bitsy Yoga* twice a week, once with each child. Sarah repeatedly tells me how much she enjoys the quality one-on-one time she finds with her children during *Itsy Bitsy Yoga* classes.

A strong parent-child bond in the early years of life is where trust and a solid emotional foundation are developed. Bonding enables you to see and hear what your toddler truly desires to share with you and the world. Help your child find her passion through yoga, so that you may support her as she grows and cultivates her passion and lives a rich and meaningful life.

chapter 2

How to Use This Book

● ● ●

n this book, you will find ten practical and playful *Itsy Bitsy Yoga* routines to enjoy with your almost two- to five-year-old child. The routines are

- Wake n' Stretch Yoga
- Patience Please Yoga
- Run, Rock n' Roll Yoga
- Building Balance Yoga
- Tantrum Taming Yoga
- Strong n' Sweet Yoga
- Coordinated n' Confident Yoga
- Quiet Time Yoga
- Blissful Bedtime Yoga
- Super-Duper Yoga

Each routine includes six or seven poses that make everyday activities such as waiting, soothing tantrums, going to bed, and learning more fun for your children and easier for you too! You will discover key components within each *Itsy Bitsy Yoga* pose. The key components make learning yoga at home fun and easy! They are

- Little Spirita
- Watch Me
- Say n' Play
- On the Go with Helen
- Yogi Wogi Says
- Super-Duper Poses
- At-a-Glance Reference Charts

Now, let's take a closer look at *Itsy Bitsy Yoga*'s components.

Meet Little Spirita

 Hi! My name is Little Spirita. At the beginning of each Itsy Bitsy Yoga pose, I playfully express the pose's benefits to you. If you listen carefully, you'll find the voice and wisdom of toddlers and preschoolers within my words.

☼ Watch Me ☼

The Watch Me section provides simple directions on how to effectively demonstrate each pose for your toddler or preschooler. When I first show a young child a new pose, I begin by bringing myself into the pose. Toddlers need to see you do something before they jump in and do it too. For instance, I do not wait until after a toddler joins me on all fours to show him the Table pose. I just do the Table pose and expect that he will join me as soon as he's ready. The more yoga you do, the more yoga your child will practice too! Toddlers and preschoolers learn by mimicking, so it is essential that you perform the poses.

☯ Say n' Play ☯

Even though I love to talk and talk, I learn best when spoken to in short sentences of three to five words. I am able to understand and respond to a sentence like, "Touch your toes." But it may be hard for me to respond to a sentence like, "Reach down and touch your toes." You see, since I am so young, I can respond to only one request at a time.

Itsy Bitsy Yoga's Say n' Play technique combines developmentally-based yoga movements with toddleresque words. The Say column gives you the precise words to say to your toddler as you teach them *Itsy Bitsy Yoga*. The Play column details the corresponding physical actions. The Say n' Play makes it easy for you to have fun sharing yoga with your young child.

After demonstrating a pose to your toddler or preschooler during the Watch Me section, invite your child to join you for the fun and engaging Say n' Play. Many times, the Say n' Play builds on the Watch Me section by providing you with more detail on the action, or emphasis, of each pose. For example, here are a few lines from Say n' Play for Twisting Cow pose:

☯ Say n'	Play
Ready.	You and your toddler begin on hands and knees.
Twist.	Turn your head to the left side.
Cow!	Look back over your left shoulder.
Moo!	Settle into the twist by bringing your left shoulder closer to your stationary left hip.
Mmm…	Inhale loudly as you return to the center.

How you present the Say n' Play is important. So let's talk about eye contact and your voice. Before you begin to follow the Say n' Play, establish eye contact with your child. Your toddler will love the attention eye contact offers, and in turn, he'll be more cooperative and eager to learn.

During the Say n' Play, your voice should be chipper, yet slow and exaggerated. A playful vocal tone in the Say n' Play helps to keep your child focused on yoga. And the short phrases in the Say column help your toddler follow directions.

For your toddler, *Itsy Bitsy Yoga*'s Say n' Play can instill confidence through predictable routines, boost learning power, increase language skills, and set a yogic pace (or tempo). For adults, the Say n' Play puts you in the moment with your child. You'll notice how the Say n' Play deepens the bond and understanding you share with your child. When teaching, I often hear three- and four-year-olds singing the words of a Say n' Play along with me and their parents. I've also found that toddlers love to teach yoga as much as they love to do yoga! I hear stories from parents about how their toddler used the Say n' Play while teaching their dolls or stuffed animals *Itsy Bitsy Yoga*.

If at any time during the Say n' Play you notice that you need to gently support or encourage your child as he or she becomes familiar with the poses, please do so. Accept as perfect any pose or movement that your child produces—even if his Tree pose, for example, doesn't look quite like your Tree pose. In addition, let your toddler or preschooler decide how long to hold a pose, but in your mind try to follow the suggested number of repetitions included in the Say n' Play section. With continued practice and positive feedback from you, a child's rendition of the poses will begin to look more like the traditional yoga poses performed by an experienced Yogi. As a parent, you know what is best for your child. The awareness that Say n' Play offers helps you be more present in your child's life—even when you are not doing yoga!

On the Go with Helen

Since I have a toddler at home, I have plenty of quick tips and tricks that will help you bring yoga off the mat and into your daily routines or caregiving activities. Each pose offers a corresponding On the Go with Helen tip to make your life as a parent or caregiver easier. These tips give you a glimpse of how I share yoga with my son. Yoga is embedded in our family life, not something we simply attend once or twice a week. After introducing a pose to your toddler, follow my On the Go with Helen tips to get the most from your *Itsy Bitsy Yoga* practice. The following is an example of my tip for Crane pose.

 I use Crane pose to encourage my son to lift a foot while I put on his pants, socks, or sneakers. Say "Crane pose" and your toddler will knows it's time to lift a leg for dressing. Crane pose makes getting dressed fun and easier too!

♡ Yogi Wogi Says ♡

Yogi Wogi says is my favorite way to playfully challenge older toddlers and preschoolers. Yogi Wogi Says allows three- and four-year-olds to go deeper into a pose or experience it in some new and exciting way. Yogi Wogi Says builds upon what is taught in a Say n' Play. Young children are always learning, so it's important to share Yogi Wogi Says to keep their interest and help them excel. You may already be familiar with Tree pose, so I will share the Yogi Wogi Says from that pose.

♡ Yogi Wogi says, let's do Counting Tree! While remaining in Tree pose, count aloud with your child. One tree; two trees; three trees; and so on. Whenever you (or your child) fall out of the pose, it's time to begin again. Or you can move on to the next pose. Counting Tree teaches your toddler to strive for excellence while practicing acceptance.

✿ Super-Duper Poses ✿

In this book, you will discover eleven Super-Duper poses. Super-Duper poses bring wandering toddlers and preschoolers right back into the practice of yoga—willingly! Super-Duper poses are parent-proven to turn tears into smiles and tantrums into laughter. These poses are the counterpart to Magic Poses from my first book on yoga for babies and young tots. For easy reference, I've included a chart on pages 207–208 indicating the names, photos, and page numbers where you can find the Super-Duper poses. The next time your child starts to lose it, let a Super-Duper pose smooth over his or her frustration.

At-a-Glance Reference Charts

At the ends of chapters 4 through 12, you will find a chart of the poses within that chapter's routine. The chart consists of the name and a small photo of each pose as well as the page number for easy reference, and shows you the sequence of poses in the chapter. As your family's *Itsy Bitsy Yoga* practice continues, you might find that you can refer to the chart instead of the text in the chapter when performing some or all of the poses.

chapter 3
Fundamentals of Toddler and Preschooler
Itsy Bitsy Yoga

● ● ●

I tsy Bitsy Yoga is a wonderful way to help your young child learn about her body's capabilities. The routines involve practicing yoga while seated, standing, lying down, and on all fours. Each routine has a variation of positions, so if your toddler isn't interested in sitting down, you can move on to the next pose in the routine and come back to skipped poses at the end of the routine or a little later in the day.

Your child's yoga practice will appear different than yours. I'll teach you and your toddler or preschooler playful ways to come into more traditional yoga poses. At times, I have created new poses designed to positively affect the physical, social, and emotional health of your child. My goal is to strengthen your bond and to make everyday tasks, such as getting dressed, easier and more fun through yoga.

The more fun you have doing *Itsy Bitsy Yoga* with your child, the more fun your child will have too!

The *Itsy Bitsy Yoga* Equation

When learning how to introduce yoga to your toddler or preschooler, you'll find the following *Itsy Bitsy Yoga* equation and its explanation helpful:

$$\text{See} + \text{Understand} = \text{Do}$$

See: Young children need to see a pose. Position yourself in a way that your toddler can best see the action or the emphasis of the pose as well as your face. Your child also needs to know that you see them too! So be sure to establish and maintain eye contact with your child as you proceed through each pose.

Understand: Kids need time to understand, or comprehend, the pose. During the Say n' Play, you'll notice that I tend to repeat directive statements several times. These repetitive statements allow toddlers enough processing time to understand my words.

Do: Lastly, kids need time to do the pose, or react. During the doing stage, you can give your child encouragement or assistance as needed. Remember to keep doing the pose yourself too!

Toddler See, Toddler Do

Perform each pose in such a way that your child can imitate you. Even if you are a skilled yoga practitioner, I'd still like you to follow the Watch Me directions so that you don't overdo a pose, that is, take a pose beyond your toddler's comprehension level or physical ability. *Itsy Bitsy Yoga* is an effective program because it's simplified enough so that even the youngest toddlers can comprehend and learn new developmental movement skills. For example, if you swan dive (standing with your feet a small distance apart as you float your arms outward and hinge forward at the hips) into the Rag Doll pose, your toddler won't. Why? Developmentally speaking, swan diving into a standing forward bend is beyond the physical capability of most toddlers and preschoolers. However, your young one would be delighted to bend his knees and reach down to touch his toes and later straighten his legs. The destination remains the same, but I changed the journey so that your toddler can join you each step of the way.

If a toddler or preschooler is asked to do something she cannot do, she will not do it. Most young children would rather not cooperate if there is a strong possibility that they won't be successful. In *Itsy Bitsy Yoga,* my goal is to teach you how to show your young child how she *can* do yoga.

Your Child Will Surprise You

Because toddlers tend to learn slowly, you may feel like they are not getting it, but in fact they are. They are just busy trying to build the yoga poses from the inside out. At other times, you may be sharing a routine with your toddler and she will appear to be occupied by something else, but she may very likely be absorbing everything you are showing her. Either of these scenarios can lead to what I call spontaneous yoga, which happens hours or days after you've shared a routine with a toddler. It's when your toddler spontaneously does several amazing yoga poses out of the blue.

Many times when a toddler is learning something new, he needs to watch you do each pose slowly and repeatedly before giving it a whirl. Each time you begin a new *Itsy Bitsy Yoga* routine with your toddler, be happy if she does half of the poses you show her.

A good motto is, "The younger the toddler, the more slowly you should move through a routine." Take notice of what pose has your younger toddler's interest and allow him extra time to master the pose he seems most interested in at that moment. Challenge a preschooler's developmental skills with Yogi Wogi Says. And Yogi

Wogi Says will also keep your smart preschooler interested in yoga and learning.

Dressing for Yoga

For yoga, you and your toddler can wear anything that is comfortable and easy to move in. A toddler's toes are so expressive and vital in balancing activities, so please remove all socks and footwear if you are planning to do an entire routine.

Props

You don't need any special props to share *Itsy Bitsy Yoga* with your toddler. In some poses, I recommend incorporating stickers or your child's favorite stuffed animal or doll. That, along with some patience and enthusiasm, is all you'll really need!

A Cleared Space

You can practice *Itsy Bitsy Yoga* with your toddler or preschooler just about anywhere. At home, you may want to practice yoga in your child's bedroom rather than in the playroom. Lessening the amount of surrounding toys and other distractions can help keep your toddler engaged. If the location you choose doesn't seem to be working out, try another room. One of my favorite places to do yoga with my son is in my backyard. Mother Nature makes a beautiful backdrop for yoga and soothes the senses.

Ideally, you and your toddler will have at least a four-by-six foot space to practice in. The most important thing about the space you and your toddler use for yoga is that it be open and clear of items your toddler can bump into or trip over.

Set the ambience of your yoga space to include things that relax you and your toddler. Make your toddler's yoga practice special with fragrant incense, dimmed lights, and relaxing music.

The Whole Room Is the Yoga Mat

As a mother, I want my toddler to know that he can do yoga anywhere, anytime. A moving child already has enough boundaries. Why give them yet another boundary by practicing on a mat? When sharing yoga with my son and others, I view the entire room as our yoga mat. This allows me to let go of where yoga happens.

Once you and your toddler are familiar and comfortable with a pose, follow the On the Go with Helen tips to learn how to take *Itsy Bitsy Yoga* off the mat and into daily activities or caregiving tasks. This is how you and your child can reap the most joy and rewards from your *Itsy Bitsy Yoga* practice. I believe that yoga for this age group is *not* about how many consecutive minutes your toddler can do yoga, but about how much joy, strength, and comfort your child can find in any moment and anywhere through yoga.

How to Begin

When possible, take a few minutes to read and practice the poses on your own in advance. Having this basic familiarity will allow you to focus on your child when you practice together. Your toddler will sense your comfort and find it easier to learn yoga from you.

Sometimes the time of day and your toddler's energy level will determine what routine to practice. If your toddler seems up for anything, begin with the first routine presented in this book, Wake n' Stretch Yoga (chapter 4).

Because toddlers thrive on repetition, you may want to stick with a routine for a week or two before introducing a new routine. Your instincts (or your toddler) will let you know when it is time to explore a new pose, variation, or routine. Each *Itsy Bitsy Yoga* routine has a different flavor, so you may find that your toddler prefers, for example, my Run, Rock n' Roll Yoga routine over the Patience Please Yoga routine. Because every child is different, I don't expect your toddler to love all the poses in this book. After you and your toddler have done a majority of the poses in this book, I imagine your toddler will be directing you on which pose to do next or again!

Your toddler can practice yoga once or several times a day. Try to incorporate yoga into a specific time of day or activity. Then, each day at that time or during that activity, your toddler will come to expect to do *Itsy Bitsy Yoga* with you. On busier days, follow the On the Go with Helen suggestions to sneak yoga and affections into caregiving.

After you and your toddler become familiar with a routine, use the chart found at the end of each chapter. When you reach this point the routine will last about eight minutes. However, the exact duration of the practice truly depends on your child's learning style and mood. Some days, your child may want to skip a pose, and other days she may want to do the same pose for ten minutes!

Belly Breathe

Many *Itsy Bitsy Yoga* activities, especially Count n' Breathe (page 55), encourage deep belly breathing. Believe it or not, your toddler may find it easier to learn deep breathing techniques than you! That's because young bodies have not endured the stress and limitations that we have acquired over our lifetime. If you are not familiar with belly breathing, I'd like to teach it to you now.

Sit comfortably with a tall, erect spine. Your toddler can watch you or be in another room. Shrug your shoulders up and then roll them down and back. This invites your chest to open (freeing the love and energy in your heart to shine and expand). Place your hands on your thighs with your palms up. Bring your elbows in, close to your sides, and your shoulders down. Breathe in and out through your nose, using long, deep, and slow breaths.

As you inhale, fill your tummy, like a balloon. Continue inhaling until you have completely expanded your chest as well. Now, "sip" in even more air. Feel your lungs expand! Pause and hold without locking up. (If you are pregnant, do not hold your breathe.) Gradually, increase the time you hold the inhale from a few seconds to up to a minute as you progress in your practice.

Exhale completely. Empty yourself of breath by contracting your hips, then your abdominal region, and finally your diaphragm. Let your heart feel like it is simultaneously pressing toward your spine and down toward your belly button. Squeeze it all out!

Do this three to eleven times before each yoga practice or anytime your toddler is wearing you thin.

Set Your Intention

The subconscious mind is like a computer; it does and believes what is entered. The words you say to your child become her internal script or dialogue. For that reason, create a positive intention before practicing *Itsy Bitsy Yoga*. You can choose one of the intentions I have provided or make one up with the assistance of your preschooler:

I am special!
My body is amazing!
You are the best you!
I am happy and playful!

Honor the Body and Embrace Its Limitations

Please note that if you feel pain or discomfort when practicing a pose, you should stop! If you have a medical condition or physical ailment that might affect your ability to practice yoga, please get permission from your medical professional to practice the poses in this book. If your child has any medical issues or conditions, you must present this book to your child's medical team for clearance before practicing the poses with your child at home.

Healthy toddlers and preschoolers have a built-in mechanism that will tell them to move away from anything that doesn't feel good. A toddler or preschooler will not put herself into a position that is uncomfortable. If she does find any discomfort at any time during a pose, she is likely to come out of the pose. If she instead tells you about her discomfort, you should invite her out of the pose.

Give Praise

Young children who receive praise for the yoga poses they do will continue to do yoga. Praise the actions you want your toddler to repeat; ignore anything you do not want your toddler to repeat. When practicing yoga with your child, describe your child's appropriate behavior by verbalizing his or her actions and incorporate any physical gestures that may help your toddler into a pose. For instance, suppose you are lifting your leg into the Tree pose. You can take this a step further by also imitating your child's behavior while describing it.

You can praise and encourage your toddler not only with words but also with physical expressions, such as a smile, nod, high-five, pat on the back, or thumbs-up sign.

For added success in sharing *Itsy Bitsy Yoga* with your young child, do the following:

- Give rewards immediately after the activity or behavior you want to increase.
- Initially, reward the activity or behavior every time it occurs.
- Reward only the activities or behaviors you want to increase.

- Sit, kneel, or lean so that your face is slightly below your child's level as you offer praise and encouragement.
- Imitate your child's movement or behavior or pose.
- Follow *Itsy Bitsy Yoga*'s Say n' Play technique to reduce directions and questions.

Follow Your Toddler's Agenda, Not Yours

One of the biggest mistakes anyone can make when sharing yoga with toddlers and preschoolers is to stick to an agenda that is not child-centered. This yoga practice is theirs; not ours. Let your toddler direct you into the routine that would work best for him or her in this moment. For instance, if your toddler is all over the place, begin with the Run, Rock n' Roll Yoga routine instead of Patience Please Yoga. Begin where your toddler is. From there, you will be able to guide your toddler into the poses or routine you want to practice.

Repeat the Poses

Toddlers learn through repetition, which develops memory and comprehension. Toddlers want to show us how capable they are. As your child becomes familiar with a pose and its Say n' Play, they'll anticipate, or predict, what comes next. Correct predictions lead to a child who is happier, confident, and smarter too!

Refine in Time

As your toddler jumps into Warrior pose, for example, you may notice it is not as strong and aligned as your Warrior pose. That is absolutely fine. I believe if a toddler puts herself into a pose, she is comfortable as is. A toddler is wired to reposition herself whenever she becomes uncomfortable. For now, find something you like about your toddler's rendition of Warrior and offer her praise. Soon your toddler will build confidence in each pose. That's when you can begin to offer subtle suggestions to help refine her posture. In the Yogi Wogi Says and On the Go with Helen sections, you'll notice that I've included lots of playful ways to assist your toddler into a more traditional pose.

Involve Siblings

If your child has a baby brother or sister, practice "I'm a ..." pose on page 133. It's a warm way for your toddler to welcome a newborn into the family. You may also want to purchase a copy of my first book, *Itsy Bitsy Yoga: Poses to Help Your Baby Sleep Longer, Digest Better and Grow Stronger*. It provides seventy-five poses to share with your baby or young tot. Big brothers and sisters can be a useful impetus for a toddler who is learning yoga. In a number of poses, I give fun suggestions on how to include other siblings and grownups in your toddler's very special *Itsy Bitsy Yoga* time.

End with a Short and Sweet Relaxation Activity

At the end of any *Itsy Bitsy Yoga* routine, share one of the following relaxation treats with your toddler:

- Sing the "Special You" song (page 200) to your toddler.
- Share an Om-az-ingly (page 181) sweet affirmation with your child.
- Play whatever music relaxes you as you lie down and rest with your toddler.

- Take your toddler on a nature walk. A few blades of grass or a tree can fascinate a toddler, so going to a local park or your backyard will suffice.
- Give your toddler a massage. Then teach your toddler how to rub your back!
- Practice your yoga in front of your toddler and let her join you in any way she wants.
- Read a book that seems to make the world a better place. Many books teach peace and promote love, kindness, gratitude, oneness, and respect for nature. E-mail books@itsybitsyyoga.com for a current list of my personal favorite toddler and preschool books!

My Top Ten Tips for Teaching Your Toddler or Preschooler *Itsy Bitsy Yoga*

Following are the ten tips that I consider important as you embark on sharing yoga with your child:

1. Practice yoga routines in a safe and relaxing part of your home.
2. Do the routine that best fits the moment and your child's needs.
3. Make the whole room the yoga mat.
4. Provide simple directions.
5. Model the poses and actions you desire.
6. Vary your energy to match the energy level of your child.
7. Mirror your child's words and movement.
8. Encourage and acknowledge creativity.
9. Reward appropriate behavior.
10. Be specific when you praise your child.

chapter 4

Wake n' Stretch Yoga

● ● ●

The Wake n' Stretch Yoga routine is a fun series of warm-up poses to start the day or begin your yoga practice. The routine consists of the following poses:

- The first pose in this routine is Table pose, which strengthens the arms, torso, and legs.
- Playful poses such as Cat and Cow warm up the spine. And the animal noises I'll ask you to make during them tend to grab the attention of toddlers.

- Twisting Cow, along with the other poses in this routine that are practiced on hands and knees, helps strengthen a young child's fine motor skills.
- Child pose is great for digestion and self-soothing. At home, I ask my son to go into Child pose instead of putting him into a time-out. Child pose calms my son and keeps his self-esteem intact.
- Down Dog strengthens the upper body and helps winded toddlers catch their breath. It's a favorite too! I have not met a young child who doesn't love Down Dog pose!
- Lunge pose requires a little more effort than the rest of the poses in this routine, but its rewards are a boost in your toddler's coordination and confidence!

Because Wake n' Stretch Yoga may be the first routine you are embarking on with your toddler, I want to remind you that your child may at first just want to *watch* you do the poses—and that's fine. In a matter of minutes, your toddler will begin to mimic you and joyfully move into the yoga poses. During a routine, give your toddler lots and lots of encouragement. Not only are you your toddler's first teacher, you are your toddler's first best friend! The encouragement you give your child during yoga (or anything else for that matter) will boost his confidence. Let your toddler know that he can do it!

Table

Wake n' Stretch Yoga

• • •

 Table pose was a popular position when I was crawling, but now that I am walking and running I have forgotten how good Table pose feels! Table pose strengthens my arms, legs, and torso. It also helps bring an awareness and connection to the core of my being.

Watch Me

1. Start on your hands and knees.
2. Place your palms shoulder-distance apart on your mat. Space your knees and feet hip-distance apart.
3. Spread and press your fingers onto the floor. Align your hands so that each middle finger is pointing forward.
4. Inhale as you flatten your back like a table.

NOTE: If you have wrist issues, you can use your fists rather than your open palms.

⑥ Say n' Play

Come on your hands and knees.	Let your toddler mimic you as you come onto your hands and knees.
Table pose, Table pose!	Check hand, knee, and feet placement for proper distance.
Breathe into your belly.	As you inhale, broaden your back.
Fill your belly.	Continue to inhale as your arms press into the floor.
Nice flat back, Table pose!	Exhale. Cheer for your toddler!

On the Go with Helen

 I love to share Crawling Table (detailed next in Yogi Wogi Says) with my son. The benefits of Crawling Table may include improving forthcoming writing, reading, and learning skills.

♡ Yogi Wogi Says

Yogi Wogi says, give someone a ride on your back in Crawling Table. Let your toddler choose a small stuffed animal. Place the stuffed animal on your toddler's back, directly above her belly button. This helps bring awareness and breath to her core. Now, invite your toddler to crawl behind you with the stuffed animal balanced on her back. Once the stuffed animal falls, ask her if she wants you to put it on your back for a ride. This instills taking turns and promotes teamwork.

Cat

Wake n' Stretch Yoga

● ● ●

Cat pose is a meow-arvelous stretch that teaches me how to initiate movement from my center. Cat pose combined with Cow pose awakens the circulation through my spine and core so I feel healthy and ready for a good day. Cat pose also stimulates the digestive tract, which may help me eat a better breakfast!

☀ Watch Me

1. Begin on all fours as in Table pose. Palms are shoulder-distance apart. Knees are hip-distance apart and positioned directly under your hips.
2. In Cat pose, lower your chin towards your chest as your tailbone tucks under. Your spine arches upward like a cat.
3. Press your hands into the floor so your shoulders stay lifted. Feel the rounding of your spine as your midback reaches up to the sky.

NOTE: If you have wrist issues, you can use your fists rather than your open palms.

⑥ Say n' Play

Look at your belly.	Exhale as your head drops down between your arms and your tailbone tucks under.
Meow!	Press your hands into the floor so your shoulders stay lifted. Feel the rounding of your spine as your midback reaches up to the sky.
Mmm …	Breathe in deeply. As you inhale, return to Table pose, or combine Cat with the next pose, Cow.

Repeat eight to twelve times.

On the Go with Helen

 On most mornings, I share Cat pose with my toddler. I find doing the entire Wake n' Stretch routine establishes a loving connection with my son and helps us stretch our way into a new day together!

♡ Yogi Wogi Says

Yogi Wogi says, with your head down between your elbows in Cat, slowly turn your head from side to side several times. This action helps release tension in the jaw and neck.

Cow

Wake n' Stretch

• • •

 When I combine Cat and Cow, I learn how to coordinate my breath with movement (a theme in all yoga poses). Cow pose in particular creates a safe backward-bending movement for me. This pose also helps free tension in my neck and shoulders.

☼ Watch Me

1. Begin on all fours as in Cat or Table pose. Your palms are shoulder-distance apart. Your knees and feet are hip-distance apart.
2. In Cow, tilt your hips and nose upward as your belly button presses downward.

NOTE: If you have wrist issues, you can use your fists rather than your open palms. Also, if you are pregnant, do not lift your head upward in Cow. Instead, keep your head and eyes parallel with the floor to avoid straining your abdominal muscles.

⑥ Say n' Play

Look up, head up.	Inhale as you slowly float your head and hips up to the sky.
Mooooo!	Exhale, pressing your belly button towards the floor. Press your hands into the floor as you gently reach higher through your head and tailbone.
Mmm ...	Inhale deeply as you return into Table pose or return into Table, then Cat.

Slowly repeat eight to twelve times.

On the Go with Helen

 When I practice yoga with my son, we often pretend to be different animals. Embodying animals is a wonderful way to foster your child's love, respect, and compassion for the animal kingdom.

♡ Yogi Wogi Says

Yogi Wogi says, how many different things can you and your child do to act like a cow? Can you eat hay like a cow? Can you make milk like a cow? Can you walk like a cow? This kinesthetic learning experience will bring animals and their attributes to life for your child.

Twisting Cow

Wake n' Stretch Yoga

• • •

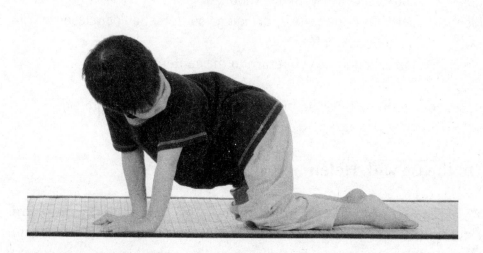

 The entire Wake n' Stretch routine is packed with poses that help me bear weight into my palms. These poses not only wake my body, they boost the fine motor development skills I need to button my clothes, zip my jacket, and hold a crayon. Thanks to Itsy Bitsy Yoga's *Wake n' Stretch routine, I can start my day right and know I'm well-prepared for preschool and kindergarten!*

☼ Watch Me

1. Twisting Cow offers a sideways stretch of the spine and torso.
2. To twist your cow, come onto all fours.
3. Level your back as in Table pose and look over one shoulder. Your hips can stay in place as you twist towards the shoulder you're looking over.

⑥ Say n' Play

Ready.	You and your toddler begin on hands and knees.
Twist.	Turn your head to the left side.
Cow!	Look back over your left shoulder.
Moo!	Settle into the twist by bringing your left shoulder closer to your stationary left hip.
Mmm …	Inhale loudly as you return to the center.

Repeat one to three times before twisting your cow to the right side.

On the Go with Helen

I discovered that I can brush my son's hair without complaints while he's doing Twisting Cow. At one time or another, your toddler too has probably refused to have his hair brushed. If that happens again, sit across from your child while he's in Twisting Cow. You can then easily brush all sides of his head. I like to remind my son that animals get brushed too and enjoy being groomed!

♡ Yogi Wogi Says

Yogi Wogi says, can your toddler see you when he twists back? Make a little game out of Twisting Cow by doing it directly behind him. Let his toes touch your toes as you line up. Notice what side your toddler's head is turning to and follow suit. Moms and Dads, look who you can see in Twisting Cow!

Child

Wake n' Stretch Yoga

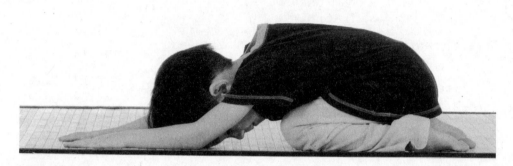

 Sometimes I like to sleep in Child pose. Once you discover the contentment that Child pose brings, you'll understand why! Child pose also helps ease constipation troubles.

☀ Watch Me

1. From Table pose, drop your bottom to your heels.
2. Stretch your arms as far forward as possible.
3. Invite your forehead to rest on the floor.

NOTE: If you are pregnant, make space for your baby belly in Child pose by spreading your knees apart and allowing the sides of your big toes to touch.

⑤ Say n' Play

Sit on your feet   From Table pose, show your toddler how to drop her bottom to her heels.

like this.	Demonstrate again. If needed, you can use one hand to gently guide your child's bottom to her heels.
Now, stretch your arms.	Extend your arms forward.
Ahhh! Child pose.	Rest peacefully in Child pose for as long as your toddler desires.

Repeat one to three times.

On the Go with Helen

 I put my toddler into Child pose instead of using time-outs. Child pose pacifies the whole body and gives him a tool to self-soothe, or calm himself.

♡ Yogi Wogi Says

Yogi Wogi says, let's rub mommy's back! Let me show you how. While your preschooler is in Child pose, rub her back with one hand. Now come into Child pose and ask her to reciprocate.

☀ Down Dog ☀

Wake n' Stretch Yoga

• • •

 Down Dog is an all-time favorite! It's good for me—it gives my brain a boost in circulation, improves breathing, and strengthens my upper body. And grown-ups love Down Dog because it removes fatigue and rejuvenates the body—something parents of toddlers need!

☀ Watch Me

1. In Down Dog , you'll make a triangular shape with your body. It's best to give your toddler a profile of the pose as you demonstrate it.
2. Begin in Child pose. This sets the proper hand and foot alignment for Down Dog.
3. As you inhale, lift your head and hips upward, passing through the Cow pose.

4. Begin to exhale as you curl your toes under and straighten your legs.
5. Press your hands downward into the floor. Also press your heels down for a nice Down Dog stretch!
6. Say hi to your toddler before you lower out of Down Dog pose.
7. Now it's time to get your toddler involved with the Say n' Play.

NOTE: If you are pregnant (or if Down Dog challenges you), widen the distance between your feet and bend your knees.

⑤ Say n' Play

Watch me, Down Dog!	From Child pose, float up into Down Dog.
(Child's name) watch me, Down Dog!	Hold Down Dog and make eye contact with your toddler.
	Slowly lower down.
You try, you try Down Dog!	Repeat Down Dog as you encourage your toddler to try the pose with you!
Down Dog!	If needed, give your toddler assistance by helping him lift his bottom up.
That's it! (or Almost!)	Clap and cheer!

On the Go with Helen

Transform Down Dog pose into a tunnel your toddler can crawl through. For even more fun, gather the entire family to make a really long tunnel. The adults and teens can line up their hips and hands in Down Dog pose. Then invite all the children to crawl through the Family Down Dog Tunnel!

♡ Yogi Wogi Says

Yogi Wogi says, do Down Dog under mommy or daddy. Come into Down Dog and encourage your toddler to do her Down Dog under yours. If you have several children, try a Triple Down Dog Pile by stacking the oldest over the youngest. It's healthy family fun!

Lunge

Wake n' Stretch Yoga

● ● ●

During Lunge pose I take a huge step forward with one foot while my hands remain on the floor. Lunge pose engages my balance, coordination, and strength. I can't recall ever doing something like this before! Wow! I am getting so big and strong!

☼ Watch Me

1. Start by facing your toddler in Down Dog pose.
2. During Lunge pose, note that your hands and front foot should form a horizontal line. Your chest rests on your front thigh and the back leg remains extended. Your eyes happily gaze forward at your toddler.
3. The first portion of Say n' Play will instruct you on how to properly demonstrate Lunge pose for your toddler. The second portion of Say n' Play guides you and your toddler to do the pose together.

⑥ Say n' Play

Let's do Lunge pose.	From Down Dog, look forward at your toddler.
Step one foot forward.	Step one foot forward and place it between your hands on the floor.
See one foot forward?	Stay in the pose so your toddler may observe your positioning.
See my foot between my hands?	Encourage your toddler to notice where your foot landed.
Now, you try, you try Lunge pose!	Return into Down Dog pose and encourage your toddler to do the next Lunge pose with you!
Step one foot forward.	Encourage your toddler to begin to step one foot forward.
Step one foot forward.	The foot lands close to, or preferably between, your toddler's hands on the floor.
Good step forward.	Help your toddler adjust his foot, or hands, as needed.
Good—that's Lunge pose!	Allow your toddler to hold the pose.
Lunge pose!	Let your toddler come out of Lunge any way she wishes.

On the Go with Helen

 During Lunge pose, strategically place a stuffed toy near the spot you'd like your child's foot to land. This visual placement marker will help your toddler understand exactly where to place his foot in Lunge pose.

♡ Yogi Wogi Says

Yogi Wogi says, when you come out of Lunge pose, try to step your front foot back into Down Dog. Although this is typical for adults to do in yoga, it will challenge your preschooler at first. With patience and caring guidance, young children can do almost anything—including stepping back into Down Dog from Lunge pose!

The Itsy Bitsy Wake n' Stretch Yoga Routine

Table
page 35

Cat
page 37

Cow
page 39

Twisting Cow
page 41

Child
page 43

Down Dog
page 45

Lunge
page 48

chapter 5
Patience Please Yoga

● ● ●

The activities in the *Itsy Bitsy Yoga*'s Patience Please Yoga routine can make waiting fun for your toddler and less stressful for you. Because toddlers are engulfed in the present moment, waiting for future events can feel like an eternity! Can you remember how long it took for birthdays and holidays to arrive when you were a child? And now, as gracefully aging adults, we can't believe how quickly time flies! The next time you find yourself saying "wait a minute" to your child, begin to practice a few, or all, of the Patience Please Yoga activities. By doing so, you will transform the stress and uncertainty of waiting with a toddler into learning and yogic fun.

The poses and games in the Patience Please Yoga routine follow:

- Count n' Breathe combines counting with mindful breathing to make your toddler smarter and calmer. When one of my students was learning how to use the potty, her mom used Count n' Breathe to relax her daughter while she sat on the potty and waited.
- Mountain pose can teach your toddler how to stand in stillness.
- Tree can easily turn playful by calling out "timberrrr!" Be sure to practice the Counting Tree variation too.
- Can You Wiggle? is also engaging and silly.
- My toddler often travels with me, and the Where Is ... ? and Name-O activities are some of our favorite ways to pass the time. Toddlers love the "I Spy" nature of the Where Is ... ? game. Name-O gets toddlers acquainted with letters and spelling in a rhythmic and memorable fashion.

I can count on the Patience Please Yoga routine to entertain my toddler when the novelty of crayons and Play-Doh wears out, and I am sure you will too.

Count n' Breathe

Patience Please Yoga

● ● ●

 Count n' Breathe combines mindful breathing with counting to help me grow smarter and calmer. Count n' Breathe also boosts my patience, which will help me excel in all I do!

☼ Watch Me

1. If possible, be seated with your toddler.
2. Establish eye contact with your toddler.
3. Inhale deeply through your nose and allow your breath to be audible.
4. Help your toddler notice how your breath lengthens your spine.
5. Exhale with a slight sigh and feel any tension float away.

⑥ Say n' Play

See mommy breathe!	Slowly inhale and exhale.
You try (toddler's name), you try.	Prompt your toddler to inhale and exhale like you.
You breathe!	Again prompt your toddler to inhale and exhale like you.
Breathe in; breathe in, in, in!	Prompt your toddler to inhale with you.
Breathe out; breathe out, out, out!	Prompt your toddler to exhale with you.
Good! Now let's count!	
Breathe in one!	Inhale
Breathe out two!	Exhale
Breathe in three!	Inhale
Breathe out four!	Exhale
Great! Let's do more!	
Breathe in five!	Inhale
Breathe out six!	Exhale
Breathe in seven!	Inhale
Breathe out eight!	Exhale

On the Go with Helen

Use Count n' Breathe to help your child develop an appreciation for Mother Nature. At home in our flower garden, my son and I inhale the sweet smell of flowers. Breathe in one flower; breathe out two flowers; breathe in three flowers; breathe out four flowers; and so on. If your child starts to show interest in something else, remain flexible. Begin to Count n' Breathe something else or move on to the next pose.

♡ Yogi Wogi Says

Yogi Wogi says, grown-ups relax completely when toddlers practice the Count n' Breathe exercise. Your child will benefit from witnessing your breath and deeper state of relaxation—even when it seems that she's not paying attention to what you're doing!

Mountain

Patience Please Yoga

● ● ●

 Mountain pose helps me learn how to enjoy standing still. In this pose, I get to feel big and strong! Mountain pose aligns my body to ensure that I keep standing tall as my body grows. It also increases my awareness and helps me refine my sense of balance.

☀ Watch Me

1. Stand two feet in front of your toddler.
2. Bring your feet together. Emphasize how the sides of your big toes can touch.
3. Press your palms together in front of your chest.
4. Take a deep breath in and feel your head reaching to the sky as your feet press down into the earth.

⑥ Say n' Play

Feet together!	Stand and bring the sides of your feet together so that your big toes touch.
Big toes touch! That's it!	Look down at your toes. Clap the sides of your big toes together, prompting your toddler to bring his feet together.
Bring hands together.	Press your palms together in front of your chest.
You do it.	Float your palms two inches apart.
Hands together!	Press your palms together once more.
Mountain pose!	Hold the pose.
Big breath in!	Inhale deeply as you stand tall.
Nice, tall Mountain pose!	Smile at your toddler.

On the Go with Helen

In the bathtub, I use Mountain pose to make rinsing out shampoo fun. I love to tell my son, "It's raining on Mount Andrew!"

♡ Yogi Wogi Says

Yogi Wogi says, float your hands up, up, and away like grown-ups do in Sun Salutations. From Mountain pose, show your toddler how to float her palms up past the tip of her nose, apart, and down into Mountain pose's starting position. Now, invite your toddler to do it with you by saying, "Inhale together and up!" and "Exhale apart and down!" This is a fantastic way to help your energetic child find peace and harmony!

❊ Tree ❊

Patience Please Yoga

● ● ●

 Tree pose helps me develop balance, concentration, and confidence. It's a calming pose that also strengthens my legs and feet. I just love the way Tree pose makes me feel!

☺ Watch Me

1. Stand eighteen to twenty-four inches in front of your child.
2. Place one foot on the side of your shin.
3. During Say n' Play, you may help your younger toddler find her balance by holding her hand. If you have an older toddler or preschooler, be sure to try Jumping Tree (page 122).

⑥ Say n' Play

Look, Tree pose!	Show your toddler how you lift one foot.
Tree pose!	Show your toddler how you place your lifted foot on the side of your shin.
You do.	Come into Tree pose again, but slowly, so your toddler can begin to mimic you when she's ready.
You do Tree pose!	Encourage your toddler to try Tree pose.
Lift one foot, Tree pose!	As you exhale, emphasize the lifting of one foot.
You do it, foot here, foot here!	Show your toddler where to place her foot (on the side of her shin).
That's it! Good Tree pose!	Help a younger toddler by holding her hand or connecting the lifted foot to the shin.
	If your toddler is not holding your hand for balance, you can continue.
Now bring hands together.	Press your palms together in front of your chest.
Hands together, good job!	Invite your toddler to bring her palms together too!

On the Go with Helen

You can have lots of fun pretending to fall out of Tree pose. I like to say "timber" as I (safely and playfully) fall to the floor! My son also loves to fall out of Tree pose—he thinks it's hysterical. The next time your toddler is growing impatient, try Falling Tree!

♡ Yogi Wogi Says

Yogi Wogi says, let's do Counting Tree! While remaining in Tree pose, count aloud with your toddler. One tree; two trees; three trees; and so on. Whenever you (or your toddler) fall out of Tree pose, it's time to begin again. Or you can move on to the next pose. Counting Tree teaches your toddler to strive for excellence while practicing acceptance.

Can You Wiggle?

Patience Please Yoga

● ● ●

Can You Wiggle? helps toddlers like me boost their body awareness and build strong neurological pathways. Also, wiggling tends to make me giggle!

☼ Watch Me

1. If you and your toddler are wearing socks, please take them off so you can see those toes wiggle!
2. Sit in front of your toddler.
3. Establish eye contact.
4. Be sure to let loose and have fun! Model all the wiggling for your toddler in the Can You Wiggle? pose.

♭ Say n' Play

Can you wiggle your nose?	Wiggle your nose side-to-side repeatedly.
Wiggle your nose.	Repeat.
Wiggle your nose.	Repeat.
Wiggle your nose.	Repeat.
Can you wiggle your toes?	Wiggle your toes up and down repeatedly.
Wiggle your toes.	Repeat.
Wiggle your toes.	Repeat.
Wiggle your toes.	Repeat.
Can you wiggle your knees?	Stand and wiggle your knees side-to-side repeatedly.
Wiggle your knees.	Repeat.
Wiggle your knees.	Repeat.
Wiggle your knees.	Repeat.
Can you wiggle these (fingers)?	Wiggle your fingers up and down repeatedly.
Wiggle these.	Repeat.
Wiggle these.	Repeat.
Wiggle these.	Repeat.
Can you wiggle, wiggle, wiggle?	Wiggle your entire body freely!
Wiggle as you please.	Repeat.
Wiggle as you please.	Repeat.
Wiggle as you please.	Repeat.

 ## On the Go with Helen

In addition to wiggling while waiting to promote patience, I love to do Can You Wiggle? with my son after a long car ride.

Whenever he's having difficulty falling asleep, I invite him to wiggle away any excess energy. Can You Wiggle? can help promote a night of restful sleep.

♡ Yogi Wogi Says

Yogi Wogi says, what else should we wiggle? Let your preschooler tell you what body part to wiggle next. This is a healthy way to empower her!

Where Is...?

Patience Please Yoga

● ● ●

Where Is ... ? lets me show you how sharp my memory skills are. During Where Is ... ? I identify and locate just about anything, anywhere. This game is a favorite of my friends who like "I Spy." We sing it to the tune of the "Where Is Thumbkin?" nursery rhyme.

☼ Watch Me

1. Practice this almost anywhere you find yourself waiting around with your toddler.
2. If you have an older toddler, you can pull out your favorite set of letters. During Where Is ... ?, let your toddler identify letters and help him begin to spell simple words. Now that's smart!
3. Sit comfortably with your toddler.

⑥ Say n' Play

Where is _____? *Where is _____?*	Fill in the blank with an object in the room that is familiar to your toddler.
There is _____! *There is _____!*	Let your toddler visually or physically locate the object. If needed, you can assist your toddler by singing "Could it be here? Could it be here?"
You found _____! *You found _____!*	While your toddler is pointing to or holding the located object, show your happiness for her accomplishment.
Thank you (child's name) *Thank you (child's name)*	Warmly thank your toddler for her cooperation.
What shall we find next? *What shall we find next?*	Let your toddler decide what to locate next (or make a suggestion).
Let's find _____! *Let's find _____!*	Insert the next object into the blank spot and repeat.

On the Go with Helen

Engage your toddler in a game of Where Is … ? while you are driving. Using Say n' Play, ask your child to locate easy-to-spot items such as trucks, cars of a specific color, trees, stoplights, and pedestrians. I also use Where Is … ? to entertain my son when we are shopping.

♡ Yogi Wogi Says

Yogi Wogi says, can you find me? Sing the Where Is … ? song as you play hide and seek with your toddler. Ask her to cover her eyes as you hide nearby. Keep singing so your toddler's listening ability strengthens as she works to locate you!

Name-O

Patience Please Yoga

● ● ●

 Name-O increases my ability to spell and fosters my love of letters. By using the beat of B-I-N-G-O, even the youngest toddlers can learn how to spell their names! Try it and see!

☼ Watch Me

1. Establish eye contact with your seated toddler.
2. After several repetitions, encourage your toddler to sing along.
3. Introduce Name-O to your toddler by saying, "Let's spell your name."

⑥ Say n' Play

M-A-D-I-S-O-N! (replace with your child's name)   Energetically sing the letters of your toddler's name.

M-A-D-I-S-O-N!   Continue.
M-A-D-I-S-O-N   Continue.
and Madison is your Name-O!

Repeat two to four times before changing the word.

On the Go with Helen

I like to use Name-O when eating out with my family. It is great fun for everyone to spell what was ordered for dinner! "H-O-T-D-O-G! H-O-T-D-O-G! H-O-T-D-O-G and hot dog is your dinner!" You may want to keep a menu at your table so that you can point to the letters (or pictures) of the item you chose for Name-O. Additionally, if you have crayons and paper, you can write the letters down for your toddler and point to each letter as you sing.

♡ Yogi Wogi Says

Yogi Wogi says, practice Name-O with your toddler to help him learn important phone numbers and your home address. For example, "123 Main Street, 123 Main Street, 123 Main Street in Yogaville is where I live!"

The Itsy Bitsy Patience Please Yoga Routine

Count n' Breathe
page 55

Mountain
page 58

Tree
page 60

Can You Wiggle?
page 63

Where Is ... ?
page 66

Name-O
page 68

chapter 6

Run, Rock n' Roll Yoga

• • •

The Run, Rock n' Roll Yoga routine offers active and engaging yoga poses, games, and rhymes especially for toddlers and preschoolers who prefer to be on the go! At age two, the thymus, or life gland, is at its largest size in relationship to the body. Toddlers are full of life and energy. Put your toddler's abundance of energy to good use by practicing *Itsy Bitsy Yoga*'s more active yoga poses and games. If children don't have the opportunity to release their stored-up energy, it may lead them to misbehave or settle into a sedentary approach to childhood.

The Run, Rock n' Roll Yoga routine lets busy toddlers be busy! After a burst of activity, each pose will gently guide your child to calmness and serenity. Poses within this routine can help young children find a balance between activity and rest with ease. Begin these poses with your toddler today and you may also notice how helpful the poses can be when aiding him through transitions.

Here are the poses in the Run, Rock n' Roll Yoga routine:

- During Run around Yogi, toddlers can bebop around the room—and it's actually good for their development! When your toddler turns corners and changes directions while moving, it fosters stability and challenges him.
- Star pose involves weight-shifting and improves stability. Falling Star increases flexibility and motor planning.
- Cobra and Wanna Iguana? are practiced while lying on the tummy; these poses strengthen the upper body to boost handwriting skills.
- Burrito is a Super-Duper pose! During Burrito, you get to affectionately roll your toddler into a calmer, more balanced mood.

Run around Yogi

Run, Rock n' Roll Yoga

This energetic pose helps me stay fit, learn how to follow directions, and go from busy-ness to restfulness. Each repetition of Run around Yogi teaches me how to quickly drop into a deeper, more relaxed state.

☼ Watch Me

1. Run around Yogi guides you and your toddler from fast walking to jogging to running, and then ends with a drop to the floor for R&R.
2. Before you begin this Say n' Play, clear the room of any obstacles that may end up in the way of you or your toddler.

⑥ Say n' Play

Run around yogi	In a continuous circle, walk fast with your toddler following you.
run around yogi	Repeat.
run around yogi	Repeat.
real, real slow.	Repeat.
Run around yogi	Jog in a continuous circle with your toddler following you.
run around yogi	Repeat.
run around yogi	Repeat.
real, real fast.	Repeat.
Run around yogi	Run in a continuous circle with your toddler following you.
run around yogi	Repeat.
run around yogi	Repeat.
down we go!	Both of you fall to the floor. Rest here for twenty to sixty seconds.

Repeat once or twice. Switch the direction from clockwise to counterclockwise during each subsequent repetition.

On the Go with Helen

 During Run around Yogi, I always try to sneak in a little affection after "down we go!" Moments after we fall to the floor, I ask my son, "Come over and give Mommy get-up kisses." Get-up kisses help Moms and Dads find the extra energy to do Run around Yogi all over again with their playful toddlers.

♡ Yogi Wogi Says

Yogi Wogi says, find your favorite stuffed animal. Let's do Run around Yogi with a stuffed animal in your arms! My toddler likes to offer me a stuffed animal to hold too.

Star

Run, Rock n' Roll Yoga

● ● ●

 All my toddler friends love Star pose! Its mesmerizing movement displays balance and grace as we practice shifting our weight. Through Star, we are improving many gross motor milestones, such as walking, balancing, rolling, and rocking.

☀ Watch Me

1. Stand in front of your toddler with your feet eighteen to twenty-four inches apart. Your toddler's feet should be about eight to twelve inches apart.
2. Inhale as you stretch your arms outward until they are horizontal.

3. Rock or teeter from side to side as you sing "Twinkle, Twinkle Little Star."

⑥ Say n' Play

Twinkle,	Shift your weight to the right foot, and lift the left foot to the side.
twinkle	Shift your weight to the left foot, lift the right foot to the side.
little	Shift your weight to the right foot, lift the left foot to the side.
star	Shift your weight to the left foot, lift the right foot to the side.
How I	Shift your weight to the right foot, lift the left foot to the side.
wonder	Shift your weight to the left foot, lift the right foot to the side.
what you	Shift your weight to the right foot, lift the left foot to the side.
are	Shift your weight to the left foot, lift the right foot to the side.
Up, a-	Shift your weight to the right foot, lift the left foot to the side.
bove the	Shift your weight to the left foot, lift the right foot to the side.
world	Shift your weight to the right foot, lift the left foot to the side.
so high	Shift your weight to the left foot, lift the right foot to the side.
Like a	Shift your weight to the right foot, lift the left foot to the side.
diamond	Shift your weight to the left foot, lift the right foot to the side.
in the sky.	Shift your weight to the right foot, lift the left foot to the side.

Repeat one to three times.

On the Go with Helen

You can use Star pose to help your child switch gears or activities—even when he is not willing to do so! After one or two

Star poses, you'll probably have a happier, more cooperative toddler on your hands.

♡ Yogi Wogi Says

Yogi Wogi says, if you have a hula hoop at home, use it in Star pose. Hold the hula hoop between you and your toddler at the height of your mid-thighs. Leave the inside of the hoop empty. Ask your toddler to hold the other side of the hula hoop. Now, you and your toddler can repeat Star pose's Say n' Play while holding the outer edges of the hula hoop.

Falling Star

Run, Rock n' Roll Yoga

• • •

Falling Star can increase my depth perception and improve my ability to plan movement. It also builds strength and flexibility in my feet, legs, hips, and back. (Falling Star resembles Triangle pose in yoga for adults.)

☀ Watch Me

1. Stand two to three feet in front of your toddler.
2. Come into the stance used in Star pose (page 76).
3. Do the Say n' Play for Falling Star once or twice before asking your toddler to join you. This will help her feel ready and excited to do Falling Star with you.

⑥ Say n' Play

(Falling Star to the left)

Ready!	Inhale as you space your feet wide apart.
Set!	Exhale as you rotate the left heel inward to a 45-degree angle. The right heel can be positioned at a 90-degree angle. Your toddler may not get the foot position perfect at first, and that's okay.
Go!	Inhale as you stretch your arms outward until they are horizontal.
Falling Star.	Exhale as you tilt to one side, allowing your left hand to fall close to your left foot. It's okay for the left knee to bend slightly and for the left hand to rest on the shin.
Stretch	Stretch the right hand overhead.
So good! So good!	Rest into the pose for several breaths.
Let's go to the other side.	Float up to standing. Allow your toddler to come out any way she'd like.

(Falling Star to the right)

Ready!	Inhale as you space your feet wide apart.
Set!	Exhale as you rotate the right heel inward to a 45-degree angle. The left heel can be positioned at a 90-degree angle. Your toddler may not get the foot position perfect at first, and that's okay.
Go!	Inhale as you stretch your arms outward until they are horizontal.
Falling Star.	Exhale as you tilt to one side, allowing your right hand to fall close to your right foot. It's okay for the right knee to bend slightly and for the right hand to rest on the shin.

Stretch	Stretch the left hand overhead.
So good! So good!	Rest into the pose for several breaths.

On the Go with Helen

Use Falling Star to turn clean-up chores into a game. Position your front foot behind the item you want to pick up, and then drop into Falling Star and pick the item off the floor with your lower hand. After you return to a standing position, put the item away. The more items you have to pick up, the more Falling Star you'll have to do! (This is my idea of multitasking!)

♡ Yogi Wogi Says

Yogi Wogi says, find a small toy to hold as you do Falling Star pose. The small toy will go in the hand that is reaching up to the sky. This toy gives kids something to set their gaze on as they rest in Falling Star.

☼ Cobra ☼

Run, Rock n' Roll Yoga

● ● ●

 Because I bear weight into my forearms in Cobra, it helps me strengthen the muscles I'll use when learning how to write. Cobra is a great way to strengthen my back and stretch my growing spine. It can also improve digestion, elimination, and lung capacity.

☼ Watch Me

1. Lie down on your tummy.
2. Place your forearms on the floor and align your elbows under your shoulders. Gently squeeze your elbows toward your ribs.
3. Open your palms and press all ten fingers into the floor. The middle finger of each hand should face front.
4. Press your shoulders down, away from your ears.
5. Pull your chest forward, and gaze upward.
6. Encourage your toddler to lie down like you.

Come on your belly.	Encourage your toddler to lie on her belly in front of you.
Hands go here.	Show your toddler how to put her arms and hands in place. (Refer to the preceding "Watch Me" section.)
Lift your head like me!	Extend your head and nose upward as your belly presses into the floor.
Good! Now, breathe in.	Inhale deeply.
Ready to hiss like a cobra?	Exhale as your tongue touches the back of your bottom teeth.
Mmmm...	Inhale deeply.
Hiss...	Exhale as you wiggle your head from side to side.
Mmmm...	Inhale deeply.
Hiss...	Exhale as you wiggle your head from side to side.
Mmmm...	Inhale deeply.
Hiss...	Exhale as you wiggle your head from side to side.

Continue hissing for as long as your toddler would like. When he is finished, dramatically collapse onto the floor and rest.

On the Go with Helen

When I was teaching my son how to improve his swimming by kicking his feet, I thought Kicky Cobra would help. On dry land, give Kicky Cobra a try! Come into Cobra pose. Instead of hissing, you and your toddler can flutter kick your feet as you chant "kick, kick, kicky cobra," accentuating the *k* sound. When your toddler has integrated Kicky Cobra into his movement repertoire, you can use it in the pool with him.

♡ Yogi Wogi Says

Yogi Wogi says, give your favorite stuffed animal or mommy an Eskimo Kiss! Position the receiver of your toddler's Eskimo Kiss four to eight inches in front of your toddler's nose. Both the giver and receiver reach their noses forward and wiggle their noses lovingly against each other. The Eskimo Kiss is obviously loving and kind, but it also guides your toddler into a deeper Cobra stretch.

Wanna Iguana?

Run, Rock n' Roll Yoga

● ● ●

 Wanna Iguana? is a fun way to learn Upward Facing Dog pose. As I hold my Wanna Iguana? pose, I am bearing weight into my open palms. That strengthens the muscles I'll use in fine motor skills such as handwriting. Wanna Iguana? also strengthens my arms and entire upper body. Are you ready to Iguana?

☼ Watch Me

1. Lay down on your belly, with a pathway of open space in front of you.
2. Place your fists under your chest, with your elbows bent and out to the sides.
3. Begin to army crawl for a short distance on the floor, allowing your elbows and knees to bend.
4. Encourage your toddler to come on her belly so you both can begin the fun Wanna Iguana? Say n' Play.

⑥ Say n' Play

Wanna Iguana?	Come into the starting position. Prepare to slowly count to three.
One	Begin to army crawl as one elbow and knee come forward.
two	The other elbow and knee pull the body farther forward.
three	The first elbow and knee continue to pull the body forward.
Iguana!	Press your palms into the floor, extend your arms, and pop up your head and upper body into the Iguana pose!

On the Go with Helen

 I discovered it was easier for my toddler to learn Wanna Iguana? when he had a side view of me doing the pose. Many times, toddlers need to see the length of your body (sideways) to mimic, and therefore learn, the pose.

♡ Yogi Wogi Says

Yogi Wogi says, try Wanna Iguana? the next time you are playing outside in the sun. Iguanas love sunshine, and being outside allows you to feel, smell, and hear what Mother Nature has created for us to appreciate.

☼ Burrito ☼

Run, Rock n' Roll Yoga

● ● ●

Burrito is adored equally by me and my parents. The snuggled-up feeling of Burrito calms me quickly. And this Burrito pose helps us explore sequential rolling.

☼ Watch Me

1. For Burrito, you need a yoga mat or a soft blanket. Unroll the mat or lay the blanket out on the floor.
2. Invite your toddler to lie down perpendicularly on the mat or blanket. The top of your toddler's shoulders should rest an inch *above* the top side of the yoga mat or blanket.
3. SAFETY NOTE: Be sure that you do *not* cover your toddler's face with the yoga mat or blanket.
4. When first introducing Burrito, you may want to roll up a big stuffed animal so your toddler can see what's in store for her!

⑥ Say n' Play

Come lie down; lie down here.

Place your hand where you'd like your toddler to rest.

Ready, let's roll our burrito.

Position yourself beside your toddler at the end of the mat or blanket.

Let's roll, roll, roll burrito!

Roll your toddler's torso and lower body in the entire length of the mat or blanket.

I'm going to eat you up!

For the next thirty to sixty seconds, give your burrito-ed toddler lots of love and affection while she is all bundled up!

Yum, yum, yum.

Continue.

Ready to unroll, you try.

Give minimal help but lots of encouragement as your toddler attempts to unroll herself.

Unroll, unroll.

Continue.

Nice! You did it!

Share lots of cheer and affection with your toddler.

Repeat as desired.

On the Go with Helen

Share Burrito with your child when you are helping her transition from an active state to a more centered and calm state. The next time you want your toddler off the swing set and into the house for a nap or quiet time, try Burrito!

♡ Yogi Wogi Says

Yogi Wogi says, let's roll your parent up in Burrito pose! Give it a try and see how empowering it is for your toddler to roll and eat you up! Caregivers and older siblings also make delicious fillings for Burrito.

The Itsy Bitsy Run, Rock n' Roll Yoga Routine

Run around Yogi
page 73

Star
page 76

Falling Star
page 79

Cobra
page 82

Wanna Iguana?
page 85

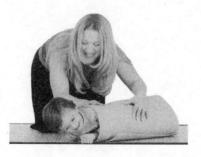

Burrito
page 87

chapter 7
Building Balance Yoga

• • •

One day while helping my toddler get dressed, I noticed that I asked him to "stand up." What I really meant was, "remain standing and keep your balance." This led me to discover that bringing yoga onto the changing table could help *us*. The Crane pose is one of my favorite ways to help my son get his feet into his pants without tipping over. Try it at home and see!

The Building Balance Yoga routine will help your child build and improve her sense of balance while seated, standing, and moving. Balance is an important skill for toddlers and preschoolers alike. It allows for the development of other skills, such as climbing and jumping. When a toddler finds balance, she feels strong and steady. However, finding a steady balance can be challenging for toddlers because they are proportioned differently than older children. Toddlers have bigger heads and relatively short legs and arms. These physical attributes combined with a reckless desire to explore their surroundings are a challenge to toddlers' sense of balance.

The Building Balance Yoga routine includes the following poses:

- Crane pose is a wonderful way to help your child gain balance while standing on one foot.
- Sunshine pose is similar to the Warrior I pose in yoga for adults. I have plenty of fun tips and tricks to help your toddler into this strong, stable, and confident yoga pose.
- March around the Zoo is an imaginative way to help your toddler become healthier and coordinated.
- Half Moon is a wonderful side-bending pose for the torso that stimulates the internal organs and increases flexibility.
- Yogi Yogi Feet is a fabulous movement rhyme that explores balance and spatial awareness.
- Rag Doll can help your toddler find focus or clarity quickly.

Crane

Building Balance Yoga

● ● ●

If you stopped to think about all the times you need me to balance throughout the day, you'd be really surprised! Crane pose helps me improve my balance. It can make daily activities, such as getting dressed, easier and fun.

☼ Watch Me

1. Invite your toddler to stand with her feet fist-distance apart.
2. Stand next to your toddler and space your feet hip-distance apart.

3. Lift one knee up to hip height. Hold the hands of a younger toddler if needed.

⑥ Say n' Play

Ready ...	Stand tall with your feet apart, and pull your tummy in.
Crane pose	Inhale as you lift one knee up to hip height.
Crane pose	Hold Crane pose. Put your hands onto your hips, or hold a younger toddler's hand.
That's it, Crane pose!	Invite your toddler to gaze at a nonmoving object to help her hold Crane pose.
Flap your wings.	If your toddler is still in Crane pose, begin to flap your arms as if they were wings. Invite your toddler to mimic you!
Good!	Lower your foot. Let both feet rest on the floor for a moment.

Repeat once before switching to the other leg.

On the Go with Helen

When helping your child get dressed, use Crane pose to encourage him to lift a foot while putting on his pants, socks, or sneakers. Say "Crane pose" and your toddler will know that it's time to lift a leg for dressing. Crane pose makes getting dressed fun!

♡ Yogi Wogi Says

Yogi Wogi says, let's count in Spanish while we do Crane pose! While holding one knee up in Crane pose, count aloud in Spanish (or another language) with your preschooler.

1. Uno crane (*oo-no*)
2. Dos crane (*dose*)
3. Tres crane (*trace*)
4. Cuatro crane (*kwat-ro*)
5. Cinco crane (*sink-o*)
6. Seis crane (*saze*)
7. Siete crane (*see-yet-eh*)
8. Ocho crane (*och-o*)
9. Nueve crane (*new-eh-veh*)
10. Diez crane (*dee-ace*)

Whenever you (or your child) drop the lifted knee and foot, it's time to either begin again or move on to the next pose. Counting Spanish Crane introduces your child to Spanish. (Or substitute Spanish with a secondary language spoken in your home.)

Sunshine

Building Balance Yoga

● ● ●

 In Sunshine I develop strength, stability, and physical confidence. (Sunshine is similar to yoga's Warrior I pose.)

 Watch Me

1. Stand across from or next to your toddler.
2. As you inhale, lift one knee up to hip height as in Crane pose.
3. As you exhale, drop the raised foot in front of you and make a big "boom" sound!
4. As you inhale, notice the distance between your front and back heel. Your feet should be spaced about a leg's length apart.

5. As you exhale, bend the front knee until it forms a right angle. Look to see that the ankle is positioned below the knee.
6. Turn your shoulders forward to help square your hips.
7. When and if your toddler appears ready, you can show her how to inhale as her arms raise overhead. To ensure good alignment, the hands should be a smidge more than shoulder-distance apart.

⑥ Say n' Play

Ready for Sunshine!	Stand diagonally from your toddler.
Lift one knee up.	Lift one knee to hip height (as in Crane pose).
Boom!	Drop the raised foot one leg's length forward and onto the floor. For toddlers, a leg length is only fifteen to thirty inches.
Good job!	Make eye contact with your toddler and check her foot and knee alignment. Give assistance as needed.
Arms up!	Float hands overhead and space them a smidge more than shoulder-distance apart.
Sunshine, sunshine.	Enjoy the pose for several breaths. Let your toddler come out of the pose in any way she wants.

Repeat, allowing the other foot to drop forward into Sunshine.

On the Go with Helen

My son now loves to do Sunshine pose with me. But when he first started, I noticed that his back heel didn't always touch the floor. Then I figured out a little trick that would help him drop the heel of the back foot. I'd invite Andrew to look back over his shoulder on the same side as the lifted back heel. The twisting motion of the uppermost torso helped drop his back heel. I have used this trick with lots of other toddlers too!

♡ Yogi Wogi Says

Yogi Wogi says, float your lifted knee and foot backwards instead of forward. Before you do, make sure the area behind you is open. This variation of Sunshine will challenge and improve your older toddler's core strength and balance.

March around the Zoo

Building Balance Yoga

After I learn how to lift my knees high, you'll see how much I love to march! March around the Zoo is an imaginative way to boost my gross motor skills and leaves me feeling healthy and strong. March around the Zoo also ties into a few other poses: Cow (page 39), Lion's Breath (page 120), and Gorilla (page 118).

☼ Watch Me

1. With arms down by your sides, demonstrate how to march with high-lifting knees.

2. Leave your arms down by your sides (don't swing them) as you teach your toddler to march.

3. Invite your toddler to march behind you.

◎ Say n' Play

March-a, march-a, march-a	You and your toddler march with high-lifting knees.
march around the zoo	Continue to march with high-lifting knees.
I see a cow!	Stop marching and establish eye contact with your toddler.
And a cow goes moo!	Come into Cow pose (page 39) and invite your toddler to do Cow too.
Moo, moo!	Do Cow pose two more times.
March-a, march-a, march-a	You and your toddler march with high-lifting knees.
march around the zoo	Continue to march with high-lifting knees.
I see a lion!	Stop marching and establish eye contact with your toddler.
And that lion is you! Roar!	Do Lion's Breath (page 120) with your toddler and invite your toddler to roar too.
Roar, roar!	Do Lion's Breath two more times.
March-a, march-a, march-a	You and your toddler march with high-lifting knees.
march around the zoo	Continue to march with high-lifting knees.
I see a gorilla!	Stop marching and establish eye contact with your toddler.
Can that gorilla be you?	Do Gorilla pose (page 118) with your toddler and make lots of silly gorilla noises.
Ooowh, ooowh!	Enjoy Gorilla pose for ten to twenty seconds.

March-a, march-a, march-a	You and your toddler march with high-lifting knees.
I love you!	Hug your toddler!

On the Go with Helen

 Share March around the Zoo with your toddler whenever he can benefit from an entertaining yet structured exercise. I find that after doing March around the Zoo, my son is more cooperative and relaxed.

♡ Yogi Wogi Says

Yogi Wogi says, lift your knees up high and swing your arms back and forth while doing March around the Zoo. I consider this variation moderate to difficult because many younger toddlers can be confused if asked to learn two new gross motor activities at one time.

Half Moon

Building Balance Yoga

● ● ●

 Half Moon pose is a wonderful side stretch. It stimulates the function of my internal organs and increases flexibility in my spine, arms, and rib cage.

☼ Watch Me

1. Invite your toddler to stand with her feet spaced fist-distance apart.
2. Stand across from your toddler with your feet together.
3. As you inhale, float your left arm upward alongside your ear with

your palm facing inward. The right arm continues to stretch down your side.

4. As you exhale, lean to the right and press your hips sideways.

5. Inhale as you float back to an upright position. Move onto the Say n' Play with your toddler.

⑥ Say n' Play

Up, up	As you inhale, one hand floats up and over your head. The other hand remains down at your side.
and away.	As you exhale, allow your torso to bend slightly.
Half Moon! Half Moon!	Rest into the pose for up to twenty-five seconds.
Breathe in.	As you inhale, float your body upright.

Repeat one to three times before switching sides.

On the Go with Helen

 Invite your toddler into Half Moon while she's seated in the bathtub. In this seated Half Moon position, encourage your toddler to cover her ear with her hand, instead of extending it overhead. I found this creative idea helps get the shampoo out of my son's hair without getting water into his ears.

♡ Yogi Wogi Says

Yogi Wogi says, stretch your fingers long and wide when you are in Half Moon. This helps you find alignment and strength as you balance in the pose. This may also help strengthen your toddler's fingers for fine motor activities such as coloring and handwriting.

✷ Yogi Yogi Feet ✷

Building Balance Yoga

● ● ●

 Yogi Yogi Feet is a fun standing pose that improves my ability to balance. Older toddlers and preschoolers can begin to learn their right from their left with your guidance during this fun Itsy Bitsy Yoga activity.

☀ Watch Me

1. Yogi Yogi Feet is *Itsy Bitsy Yoga*'s version of the "Hokey Pokey."
2. Stand next to or eighteen to twenty-four inches in front of your toddler.
3. Younger toddlers may want to hold your hand as they explore balance during Yogi Yogi Feet.
4. Begin the Say n' Play and encourage your toddler to join you!

⑥ Say n' Play

You put your left foot in.	Swing your left foot forward.
You put your left foot out.	Swing your left foot back (or to the start position).
You put your left foot in and circle it about	Swing your left foot forward. Circle your left foot in the air once before placing it on the floor.
You do the Yogi Yogi	Dance your hands up and down as in the "Hokey Pokey."
and you turn yourself around.	Twist to each side (or turn around once).
That's what it's all about!	Clap your hands together three times.

Practice Yogi Yogi Feet twice with each foot.

On the Go with Helen

I like to sing Yogi Yogi Feet to my toddler when we are stuck in traffic. It's a fun way to keep him from being completely sedentary while cooped up during a car ride that's taking longer than expected.

♡ Yogi Wogi Says

Yogi Wogi says, let's see how far your foot can go forwards and backwards in Yogi Yogi Feet. This challenges and further develops your toddler's sense of balance.

Rag Doll

Building Balance Yoga

● ● ●

 Rag Doll is a basic forward bend that provides the entire backside of my body with a great stretch. It massages my internal organs and helps blood circulate to my legs, torso, and brain.

☀ Watch Me

1. Stand three feet in front of your toddler with your feet hip-distance apart. For greater ease in Rag Doll, space your feet farther apart than suggested. For your toddler, hip-distance is about the size of an apple.
2. Check to see that your feet are parallel with one another and pointing straight ahead.

3. Now that you are ready to show your toddler how Rag Doll's Say n' Play goes, get your toddler interested in reaching for her feet. Here's why: Most toddlers will not hinge at the hip and fold forward. So when you demonstrate Rag Doll for your toddler, demonstrate how to bend your knees and slowly reach your hands down toward your toes.

⑥ Say n' Play

Ready ...	As you exhale, bend (or soften) your knees and reach down.
Bend your knees,	Encourage your toddler to bend her knees.
Bend, bend, bend your knees	As your toddler bends her knees, prompt her to also lower her hands close to her toes.
Set ... Touch your toes!	Touch your toes repeatedly.
Touch, touch, touch your toes!	Encourage your toddler to touch her toes.
Go ... Hug your elbows	Bring your hands to your elbows. Give your elbows a loving squeeze as you make eye contact with your toddler.
Hug, hug, hug your elbows!	Encourage your toddler to hug her elbows.
Wow, what a nice Rag Doll!	Let your head and arms dangle. Relax into the pose for as long as your toddler would like.

To come out of Rag Doll, bend your knees until you come down into a squat. Then when you're ready, return to a standing position and repeat.

On the Go with Helen

My toddler, like many other toddlers, loves to play with stickers. During Rag Doll, I give my son two stickers (a set for the big toes or each elbow). Then I ask him to touch his stickers to encourage him to move into the pose. This has helped him build body awareness. I love to come into Rag Doll whenever I need to recenter myself quickly. It's a great pose to do after getting worked up or anxious over something!

♡ Yogi Wogi Says

Yogi Wogi says, let's try something different and turn our rag dolls into elephants! While in Rag Doll, clasp your hands together. Keep your arms long to resemble the long trunk of an elephant. Let your arms sway from side to side and make some fun elephant noises!

The Itsy Bitsy Building Balance Yoga Routine

Crane
page 93

Sunshine
page 96

March around the Zoo
page 99

Half Moon
page 102

Yogi Yogi Feet
page 104

Rag Doll
page 106

chapter 8
Tantrum Taming Yoga

● ● ●

Almost every child has a tantrum at one time or another. Heck, even adults are known to have tantrums (but we refer to these as nervous breakdowns, exhaustion, or even depression).

Tantrums are caused by frustration, upsets, and stressful enviroments. Sometimes they happen when things do not go as toddlers would like. At other times, a tantrum can happen when toddlers become frustrated with their inability to be understood by others. It must be tough to be so little in such a big world! That's why I am dedicated to helping parents connect with and better understand their young children's needs through *Itsy Bitsy Yoga*.

The Tantrum Taming Yoga routine helps you learn how to diffuse your young child's frustration, stress, or upset through breathing and movement. The poses in this routine are energetic and vibrant. I hope they help you tame your child's tantrums quickly and effectively:

- The first pose in this routine is Silly Spins, which evokes calming and laughter almost instanteously.
- Donkey helps a toddler put her head upside down and look at things a little differently.
- Gorilla is a primitive and playful way for your toddler to move about.
- Lion's Breath is a stress and anger management tool for you and your toddler.
- For older toddlers and preschoolers, Jumping Tree is a great tantrum tamer! It roots one in the present and replaces any upset with a new confidence.
- Warrior is all about being big and strong enough to do anything. And feeling big and strong can help conquer frustration.

Once you and your toddler are familiar with the Tantrum Taming Yoga poses, practice them individually or all at once. Enjoy the magic of these poses before, during, or after a tantrum.

Following are a few tips to get the most out of the *Itsy Bitsy Yoga*'s Tantrum Taming Yoga routine:

- Be familiar with the poses before you use them in a time of frustration, stress, or upset. Young children find it difficult to learn new activities during such times.

- The more upset your toddler is, the more pronounced and lively your demonstration of the pose needs to be.
- Choose your toddler's favorite pose and keep with it. Don't give up! The more upset your toddler is, the more repetitions and time your toddler needs to notice and respond to you.

Silly Spins

Tantrum Taming Yoga

● ● ●

 I love to spin myself silly during Silly Spins! Spinning calms me very quickly—even when I am overtired or completely frustrated. Before we begin Silly Spins, my mom finds a clear and open space for spinning so no one bumps into anything while having fun.

☀ Watch Me

1. Stand near your toddler.
2. For Silly Spins, you can hold your toddler's hands and spin together. Or you and your toddler can spin independently of each other. It depends on the mood and temperant of your toddler.
3. If you and your toddler do Silly Spins *without* holding hands, spin yourself around only a few times to show your little one how much fun spinning is. Once your toddler begins to spin, you should *stop* spinning and monitor your toddler's safety.

⑥ Say n' Play

Spin,	Stand and spin clockwise once.
spin,	Continue.
silly	Continue.
spins!	Continue.
	Repeat once before continuing.
Yeah!	Establish eye contact with your toddler.
Spin the other way.	Help your toddler transition to spinning counterclockwise.
Spin,	Stand and spin counterclockwise once.
spin,	Continue.
silly	Continue.
spins!	Continue.

Repeat the counterclockwise Silly Spins once.

On the Go with Helen

I use Silly Spins whenever my son starts to show his more primitive side. Silly Spins works wonders in calming toddlers. One of the favorite pastimes for the toddlers in my house is to sit on a grown-up's lap and do Silly Spins in the office chair. My entire family loves to watch how spinning melts fussiness on the spot!

♡ Yogi Wogi Says

Yogi Wogi says, gently drop to the floor after Silly Spins. Toddlers love the drama of pretend falling. This also allows them to safely recover from any dizziness.

Donkey

Tantrum Taming Yoga

● ● ●

 I love Donkey pose! It strengthens my balance and gives me a joyful confidence. As you teach me Donkey pose, you have the opportunity to discover something about my learning style. Do I dive right in and do Donkey pose? Or do I need to watch you do the pose several times before I attempt it?

☼ Watch Me

1. Begin Donkey pose by coming into Down Dog pose (page 45).
2. When first demonstrating Donkey pose to your toddler, it is helpful to position your Down Dog pose diagonally in front of your toddler.
3. Once in Down Dog, lift one foot up to bring yourself into Donkey pose. Your hip bones should face downward as the lifted leg extends long.
4. Use the Say n' Play to encourage your toddler to do Donkey too!

Ready to do Donkey?	You and your toddler come into Down Dog.
Watch! Lift one foot,	Shift your weight so you can lift one foot into the sky.
lift one foot up high!	Extend the leg high.
You try!	Make eye contact with your toddler.
Lift one foot,	You and your toddler lift a foot into the sky.
lift one foot,	Continue.
lift one foot up high!	The toddler's leg extends high, or stop to give your toddler assistance.
That's it!	Respond positively to your toddler.
Good Donkey pose!	Clap and cheer for your toddler!

Repeat as desired.

On the Go with Helen

Share Donkey pose with your child to help her see her surroundings from a different perspective. My son loves to do Donkey on the lawn and see the grass on top of the blue sky because he's upside down. Donkey pose helps us gain perspective and develop the ability to think outside the box.

♡ **Yogi Wogi Says**

Yogi Wogi says, can you lift your other foot and leg up in Donkey pose? I notice some toddlers prefer to always lift the same leg. So, if needed, give your toddler plenty of encouragement as she attempts to lift her other leg up into Donkey pose.

❋ Gorilla ❋

Tantrum Taming Yoga

● ● ●

 When I am doing Gorilla, I need a clear pathway to travel through. Speaking of pathways, the more I toss my legs off to the sides while my hands walk forward in Gorilla, the more neural pathways I develop.

☻ Watch Me

1. From Down Dog (page 45), invite your toddler to lift her head and look forward. The chin becomes parallel with the floor.
2. Begin to show your toddler how to walk on all fours like a gorilla. Your gaze is forward. Your bottom is up high and your legs toss sideways as you propel forward.
3. Demonstrate Gorilla pose so your toddler can comprehend the movement and fun to be had!

⑥ Say n' Play

(Make gorilla sounds) Gorilla-walk freely for fifteen to ninety seconds.

On the Go with Helen

You can use the Gorilla pose to change your toddler's locale when he's more interested in staying put. For instance, if I want my son to follow me into my home office but he'd rather stay in the kitchen, I'll say, "Okay, instead of walking to my office, can you Gorilla to my office?" Many times, my son does Gorilla and it saves us from a struggle.

♡ Yogi Wogi Says

Yogi Wogi says, can you Gorilla backwards? Instead of your toddler's hands leading her forward, instruct (and show) your toddler to step her feet so they reach backwards in the Gorilla pose. Be sure your toddler's path is clear and that you are present to prevent her from crashing into an unforeseen obstacle.

Lion's Breath

Tantrum Taming Yoga

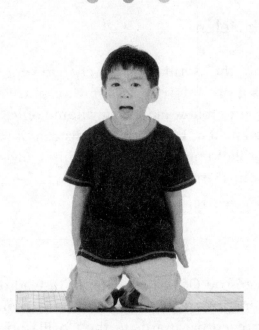

 The best way to teach me Lion's Breath is to show me how you do it rather than tell me. When you do Lion's Breath, you may feel silly at first; but it will leave you feeling rejuvenated and stress free!

☼ Watch Me

1. Kneel, sit, or stand across from your toddler and establish eye contact.
2. As you inhale, allow your head and chest to lift upward.
3. As you exhale, emit a loud, exaggerated, roaring sigh, stick your tongue out, let your jaw drop, and let your eyes pop open!
4. Now it's time for your toddler to join you in the Say n' Play.

⑥ Say n' Play

(Make deep inhaling sounds)   As you deeply inhale, float your head and chest upward.

(Exhale with exaggerated roar)   As you exhale, roar, stick your tongue out, let your jaw drop, and let your eyes pop open!

Repeat four to ten times.

On the Go with Helen

Like many other parents, I know when my child is about to do something bad. And that's the exact moment when I'll show my son my biggest Lion's Breath. Lion's Breath is the holistic way to eliminate frustration, anger, and undesirable behavior.

♡ Yogi Wogi Says

Yogi Wogi says, let's see how far you can stick your tongue out in Lion's Breath! Some of the best benefits of this pose come from a really long stretch of the tongue because it releases tension in the jaw, face, and throat.

Jumping Tree

Tantrum Taming Yoga

• • •

 Three-and-a-half-year-old Jenna invented Jumping Tree pose during an Itsy Bitsy Yoga *class. Jumping Tree has become a true delight for me and my three- and four-year-old friends! This pose helps me develop gross motor skills and improves my balance.*

☀ Watch Me

1. Stand two to three feet in front of your toddler.
2. Place one foot on the side of your shin.
3. If you have an older toddler, press your palms together in front of your chest and instruct your older toddler to do the same. Hold the hands of a younger toddler to give her support as she attempts Jumping Tree.
4. Bend your standing knee and begin to make your tree "jump" in place.

5. Have fun doing Jumping Tree for ten to thirty seconds—long enough to entice your toddler to try it!

⑥ Say n' Play

Tree pose!	Emphasize the lifting of one foot.
Tree pose!	Encourage your toddler to place her foot on the side of her calf.
Hands ready!	Press your palms together or hold a younger toddler's hands.
Watch me, Jumping Tree!	Begin to do Jumping Tree in place.
You do,	Encourage your toddler to do Jumping Tree.
you do Jumping Tree!	Continue.
Good! Jump, jump	Continue.
Jumping Tree! Wheee!	Continue.

On the Go with Helen

I like to take toddlers out to the backyard to do Jumping Tree while barefoot. This lively pose makes them feel connected to the earth that lies below their feet. When finished with Jumping Tree, we visit the wise trees in the yard. It's never too early to teach children how to honor and respect all living things.

♡ Yogi Wogi Says

Yogi Wogi says, once your toddler has mastered Jumping Tree, see if she can jump forward when doing the pose. Before you begin, clear your yoga space of any obstacles. Jumping Tree has a tendency to leave kids giddy and exhausted!

Warrior

Tantrum Taming Yoga

• • •

 Warrior (or Warrior II pose as adults who practice yoga know it) is an intense pose with lots of subtle adjustments. My toddler friends and I like to playfully jump into Warrior pose! Be accepting of whatever position I jump into. Early renditions of more challenging poses such as Warrior are fine, no matter what they look like!

☀ Watch Me

1. Stand near your toddler in Mountain pose (page 58) and inhale deeply.
2. As you exhale, jump your feet and arms out. Give the jump a "psssht" sound effect.
3. Find comfort. The knee of the front foot bends so it is aligned over the ankle. The toes of the front foot point forward. The back foot turns outward at a 45-degree angle.
4. Extend your arms long and strong. Extend your fingertips away from the body with the palms facing down. Relax your shoulders.

5. Now that your toddler has seen your Warrior pose, see if you can get him to jump into Warrior during the Say n' Play.

⑥ Say n' Play

Ready, Warrior pose!	As you inhale, stand in Mountain pose with your hands together.
Psssht!	As you exhale, jump into Warrior pose.
Warrior pose!	Invite your strong toddler to hold Warrior for as long as she'd like.

Repeat Warrior several times. The next time your toddler does the pose, try my playful ways to help her adjust her pose in the On the Go with Helen and Yogi Wogi Says sections.

On the Go with Helen

Young children like to pretend. Activate their "superpowers" as they jump into Warrior pose. To do so, first jump into Warrior in front of your toddler so that your child's front fingertips are close to yours. Then say, "Superpowers activate!" as you invite your child to touch his fingertips to yours. This helps kids find strength in arm extension and good balance.

♡ Yogi Wogi Says

Yogi Wogi says, can your knee (or toes or foot) reach to touch your favorite stuffed animal? This is one of my favorite ways to help toddlers adjust any misaligned body part that is part of the supportive foundation of Warrior.

The Itsy Bitsy Tantrum Taming Yoga Routine

Silly Spins
page 114

Donkey
page 116

Gorilla
page 118

Lion
page 120

Jumping Tree
page 122

Warrior
page 124

chapter 9
Strong n' Sweet Yoga

● ● ●

The Strong n' Sweet Yoga routine helps your toddler grow stronger physically, emotionally, and socially. You'll notice that this routine brings sweet and affectionate interactions to you and your toddler:

- Itsy Bitsy Yogi and Ring around the Yogi include movement-based rhymes you'll find only in *Itsy Bitsy Yoga for Toddlers and*

Preschoolers. Be sure to learn the words and encourage your toddler to sing along with you! Itsy Bitsy Yogi is similar to the early steps of the Sun Salutations. This pose encourages hand-and-eye coordination and brings an energized yet balanced feeling to you both.

- Lampa-oops! is a great way to improve your child's ability to jump in place and jump forwards and backwards too! As your toddler jumps, she is building an intricate web of neuromuscular pathways. I like to say, "The more your toddler jumps, the more brain power she's building."
- I'm a ... is a warm way to welcome a newborn into the family. The pose also helps your toddler set his sights on all the things he can be.
- Danda focuses on good posture and is toe-clapping fun!
- Slide builds strength in your toddler's core and upper body.

All in all, the Strong n' Sweet Yoga routine offers you quick ways to encourage gross motor development, breath awareness, and lots of parent and child bonding opportunities.

Itsy Bitsy Yogi

Strong n' Sweet Yoga

● ● ●

Itsy Bitsy Yogi calms me as I feel my body move. I sing it to the tune of one of my favorite rhymes, "The Itsy Bitsy Spider." Like many other poses, I will begin to practice it after I watch you do it several times.

☀ Watch Me

1. Stand two feet in front of your toddler.
2. Think of Itsy Bitsy Yogi as a dance for the arms and a sweet song for your toddler's soul.
3. Practice the pose sequence in the Say n' Play before asking your toddler to follow along.

⑥ Say n' Play

The itsy bitsy yogi *reached up to the stars!*	Press your palms together in front of your chest. Extend your arms up, shoulder-distance apart. Your elbows should be by your ears.
Down shone the light *that made yogi bright!*	Float both hands down to your sides. Cross your hands over your heart.
Out poured the love *and made yogi smart!*	Lower your arms down by your sides. Sweep your hands up in front of you and let your hands land on your head.
So the itsy bitsy yogi *loves with all his heart!*	Drop your arms and crunch down into a squat. Pop up energetically into a standing position!

On the Go with Helen

I practice the Itsy Bitsy Yogi sequence when my son starts a fuss. Once your toddler becomes familiar with Itsy Bitsy Yogi, use it to help him learn how to work through his emotions and calm himself.

♡ Yogi Wogi Says

Yogi Wogi says, can you sing the "Itsy Bitsy Yogi" song? To hear Helen and her friends sing it, go to www.itsybitsyyoga.com.

Lampa-oops!

Strong n' Sweet Yoga

● ● ●

Lampa *means* jump *in Sanskrit. So as you can imagine, I'll be do-ing a lot of jumping during Lampa-oops! The pose is an engaging gross motor exercise that builds my strength and coordination. Re-member to keep me safe by practicing the pose in a clear space.*

☼ Watch Me

1. Stand two to three feet in front of your toddler.
2. To safely jump up and down and later fall in Lampa-oops!, check to see that the area is clear and open.
3. If other family members or friends are nearby, ask them to join in!

⑥ Say n' Play

Lam-pa	Bend your knees and jump.
Lam-pa	Bend your knees and jump a second time.
Lam-pa-oops!	Jump up a third time and safely fall down to the floor to rest.

NOTE: The duration of rest can increase in subsequent repetitions.

Ready ...	Spring up into a standing position.
	Repeat as desired.

On the Go with Helen

I noticed that my toddler tends to get frustrated or embarrassed when he trips and falls. To help comfort his spirits and regain his confidence, I use a silly voice to ask him, "Did you Lampa-oops?" Andrew then usually smiles. Sometimes, he'll even reenact the situation and do Lampa-oops! to show he's in control.

♡ Yogi Wogi Says

Yogi Wogi says, try jumping forward in Lampa-oops! Stand next to your toddler and say "Lampa" twice as you jump in place twice. As you say "Lampa-oops," jump forward. After your toddler masters jumping in place and forward jumping, you can continue to boost his gross motor development by asking him to jump backwards as you say "Lampa-oops."

I'm a ...

Strong n' Sweet Yoga

When I do I'm a ... in front of my baby sister, it makes her smile. I start in my heart, reach up for joy, and then look down at my baby sister. (If you're an only kiddo, see On the Go with Helen.)

☼ Watch Me

1. Stand across from your toddler.
2. If your toddler has older siblings, you can guide him into saying "I'm a little brother (or sister)" instead of "I'm a big brother (or sister)."
3. Follow the Say n' Play to learn the movement sequence of this pose.

⑥ Say n' Play

I'm	Cross your hands at your chest.
a	Reach both hands up into a Y shape.
big	Swiftly drop both hands down in front of you.
brother (or sister)	Cross your hands over your thighs. Wiggle your head.

Repeat three to five times.

On the Go with Helen

Because Andrew doesn't have any siblings yet, I use this pose to make affirmations for my toddler. He'll do the movement in the Say n' Play to affirmations such as, "I am good!" "I am kind!" "I am happy!" "I am me!" What affirmations can you think of for your toddler?

♡ Yogi Wogi Says

Yogi Wogi says, what can you be? At first you can make some suggestions, but then let your toddler fill in the blanks. For instance, "I'm a dinosaur!" "I'm a princess!" "I'm a pizza man!" "I'm a mommy!"

✵ Ring around the Yogi ✵

Strong n' Sweet Yoga

● ● ●

Ring around the Yogi is super-duper fun! This may just be my favorite pose to do with you! We get to hold hands, sing, and dance to a sweet Itsy Bitsy Yoga *song.*

☼ Watch Me

1. Stand across from your toddler and hold hands.
2. The "Ring around the Yogi" song is loosely sung to the tune of "Ring around the Rosie."
3. As you move through the Say n' Play, note that you'll come down to the floor and into Table pose before the second verse.

⑥ Say n' Play

Ring around the yogi	Hold hands and walk in a continuous circle.
namaste my friends.	Continue.
Inhale, exhale	Continue.
we all feel grand!	Playfully toss your hands up overhead.

Come down into Table pose (page 35).

Love is in our hearts	March hands up and down on the floor continuously.
and our minds are full	Continue.
of peaceful thoughts.	Continue.
Om, delightful om	Continue.
life is fun!	Playfully toss your hands up overhead.

Return to a standing position.

Repeat. As you do so, alternate your walking direction so you experience walking clockwise and counterclockwise. Continue for one to three repetitions.

On the Go with Helen

 Our family opts to do Ring around the Yogi in the living room instead of watching TV or playing with toys. I know I'm my child's favorite playmate, and my son knows he is his mom's favorite playmate too!

♡ Yogi Wogi Says

Yogi Wogi says, sing the words to the "Ring around the Yogi" song with me! Many of my three- and four-year-old students begin to sing the words after a few weeks of class. It is so sweet!

Danda

Strong n' Sweet Yoga

• • •

Danda is an energetic pose that nurtures me from head to toe! When I bend forward, I find a peace as my abdominal organs, mind, and emotions are refreshed.

☀ Watch Me

1. Invite your toddler to sit with her legs together and extended.
2. Now, position yourself across from your toddler.
3. You'll notice that Danda is a toe-clapping treat, but see the Yogi Wogi Says section to learn the toe-tickling variation of Danda too!

⑥ Say n' Play

Let's	Stretch your legs out long and flex your feet.
Danda.	Inhale, allowing the crown of your head to reach tall.

Clap toes.	Clap your big toes together. Pause with excitement.
	Point your big toes outward at a 45-degree angle as the heels stay together.
Clap toes.	Continue.
Clap toes.	Continue.
Danda	Excitedly clap your hands together

Repeat the toe-clapping Danda trick for as long as your toddler likes. If you're feeling silly, double-it up! Clap your hands and toes at the same time!

On the Go with Helen

Invite your toddler to sit in Danda while you help him put his socks and shoes on!

♡ Yogi Wogi Says

Yogi Wogi says, sit across from each other so all four feet touch. Now, reach forward and tickle the tops of each other's feet. It's a giggling great forward bend! When friends and family are around, you can all sit in a star shape (so the edges of your feet touch in the middle). It's sure to be a toe-riffic treat!

Slide

Strong n' Sweet Yoga

● ● ●

 I think of Slide as the big kid version of Bridge pose. But it's more like a Reverse Plank pose that strengthens my arms and entire back-side!

☼ Watch Me

1. You can use a small stuffed animal to slide down your toddler's body during Slide pose.
2. Start by sitting in Danda pose.
3. Place your hands on the floor so they are positioned a few inches behind you.
4. Extend your arms and legs as you lift your bottom as high off the floor as comfortable.

5. Ask your toddler to slide her stuffed animal from your chest to your toes. Wheeh! Slide pose!

⑥ Say n' Play

Let's do Slide pose.	Invite your toddler to come into the starting position described in the Watch Me section.
Lift your belly and bottom,	Your toddler lifts her bottom three to six inches off the floor.
lift your belly and bottom up!	Continue.
That's it! Ready ...	Bring the small stuffed animal to your toddler's chest.
Wheeh! Slide pose!	Slide the small stuffed animal down from your toddler's chest to her toes.

Repeat or demonstrate Slide pose again.

NOTE: Your toddler's knees will likely be bent the first few times she tries Slide. It takes time for her to gain the confidence and strength to fully extend her legs. Encouragement also helps, so try asking your toddler to walk her feet forward a few inches once her bottom lifts. Lastly, some toddlers prefer to keep upright during Slide, and that's okay.

On the Go with Helen

I enjoy practicing Slide pose to tone my lower body and increase the strength in my core and upper body.

♡ Yogi Wogi Says

Yogi Wogi says, have your toddler slide her toys up your body and into a basket. Mom, come into Slide pose with a collection basket on one side of your chest. Then, invite your toddler to march her toys from your knees upward to your chest. Once the toy arrives at your chest, the toy can get tossed (or jump) into the collection basket. It's a workout for you and a fun clean-up activity for your toddler!

The Itsy Bitsy Strong n' Sweet Yoga Routine

Itsy Bitsy Yogi
page 129

Lampa-oops!
page 131

I'm a ...
page 133

Ring around the Yogi
page 135

Danda
page 138

Slide
page 140

chapter 10

Coordinated n' Confident Yoga

• • •

Coordination is defined as a harmonious combination or interaction. The poses in the Coordinated n' Confident Yoga routine will evoke a special harmony between you and your child. This routine will leave you and your toddler feeling confident and connected:

- The Coordinated n' Confident Yoga routine begins on a positive note with "I Can" Rap. The pose includes a fun-loving song that empowers children by combining coordination, movement, and affirmations.

- Stack n' Clap begins with body awareness, then introduces the concept of right and left, and leaves you and your toddler with a silly laugh.
- Whale pose is probably one of the best poses in the book for cultivating coordination. The kids love it!
- Bow pose is a soothing stretch for growing bodies—and their parents too!
- Ball pose helps toddlers build balance and explore trust.
- Boat pose builds strength throughout your child's body as well as lots of confidence.

So go ahead and practice one, a few, or all of the Coordinated n' Confident poses with your child to help her be all that you and she desire.

"I Can" Rap

Coordinated n' Confident Yoga

 "I Can" Rap has a rap beat and opens me to the world of "I can" and possibility. This fun-loving song empowers me and other toddlers; I hope that empowerment stays with us for a lifetime!

Watch Me

1. Stand across from your toddler.
2. The first time you go through the Say n' Play, don't expect anything from your toddler.
3. Before you begin it a second time, encourage your toddler to join you!
4. Your joy and silliness during this song will motivate your toddler to try it too!

✆ Say n' Play

I can breathe	Inhale.
n' wiggle.	Exhale as you wiggle.
I can breathe	Inhale.
n' giggle.	Exhale as you giggle.
I can breathe	Inhale.
n' run.	Exhale as you run in a small circle.
I can breathe	Inhale.
n' have fun.	Exhale as you do something fun!
I can breathe	Inhale.
n' do anything.	Exhale as you bring both hands to your chest.
Think	Open your left hand out to the side.
breathe	Open your right hand out to the side.
go ...	Clap your hands.
Think	Open your left hand out to the side.
breathe	Open your right hand out to the side.
go ...	Clap your hands.
Think	Open your left hand out to the side.
breathe	Open your right hand out to the side.
go ...	Clap your hands.

On the Go with Helen

 I don't like to hear my toddler utter the words, "I can't," so I wrote the "'I Can" song. Since I've started using this empowering song with my son, he's stopped saying those limiting words and finds pride in saying, "I can!"

♡ Yogi Wogi Says

Yogi Wogi says, what else can you do? Give your toddler or pre-schooler an opportunity to be silly and creative. Ask your child to show you what she can do. Insert her response into the "I Can" Rap. By doing what she does (or asks), you let her know that what she says matters. Try it several times and watch your toddler's attitude and responsiveness change for the better.

Stack n' Clap

Coordinated n' Confident Yoga

• • •

 Stack n' Clap is a playful way to boost my body awareness as I cross the midline of my body. This pose will improve my coordination and strengthen my ability to learn. It also shows me the concept of right and left.

☼ Watch Me

1. It's a good idea to rehearse Stack n' Clap several times before performing it with your toddler so you can become familiar with this beneficial movement rhyme.
2. Begin by standing across from your toddler. Now you're ready for the Say n' Play.

⑥ Say n' Play

Let's use your right hand.	Identify and make a fist with the right hand.
You put your hand left	Slide your right hand all the way to the left.
you put your hand right	Slide your right hand back to the right.
you put your hand left	Slide your right hand to the left again.
and shake it all about.	Shake your right hand.
You do the	Stack your fists and clap them together twice.
Stack n' Clap	Alternate which fist is on top and clap your fists together twice.
and sit down for a silly laugh!	Both gently fall to the floor and giggle!
Let's use your left hand.	Identify and make a fist with the left hand.
You put your hand right	Slide your left hand all the way to the right.
you put your hand left	Slide your left hand back to the left.
you put your hand right	Slide your left hand to the right again.
and shake it all about.	Shake your left hand.
You do the	Stack your fists and clap them together twice.
Stack n' Clap	Alternate which fist is on top and clap your fists together twice.
and sit down for a silly laugh!	Both gently fall to the floor and giggle!

Repeat as desired.

On the Go with Helen

While waiting in public places with your toddler, you can use the Stack n' Clap to entertain her. Because it may not always be possible to "sit down for a silly laugh," try "stretch up for a silly laugh!"

♡ Yogi Wogi Says

Yogi Wogi says, practice the Stack n' Clap with a small toy or Beanie Baby in the moving hand. Your child will find it fun to watch the toy you are holding move from right to left and left to right. This helps develop hand-eye coordination.

Ball

Coordinated n' Confident Yoga

Ball pose lets me scrunch up and give myself a big, loving hug. It's a playful way for me to pretend how to be one of my first favorite toys— a ball! Ball pose is also good for digestion and lets me explore balancing in an entirely new fashion.

☼ Watch Me

1. Invite your toddler to sit beside you on the floor. Be sure the area behind you and your toddler is clear.
2. Remain seated as you put your feet flat on the floor, with your knees bent and at chest height.
3. Make eye contact with your toddler. Then show her how to hug her thighs by wrapping and clasping your hands under your knees. Your chest should be close to your thighs as you sit small like a ball.
4. Encourage your toddler to come into Ball pose by using the Say n' Play.

⑥ Say n' Play

Let's sit like a ball!	Be seated next to your toddler with your knees up and your feet on the floor.
Sit like Mommy (or me)!	Help your toddler find her starting position if necessary.
Now, hug your legs.	Hug your legs into your chest.
Give your legs a hug,	Encourage your toddler to hug her legs into her chest.
Hug, hug!	Continue.
Good hug, nice Ball pose!	Smile and be happy with your toddler!

On the Go with Helen

I love to share Ball pose with my son in the shallow beach water. I stay beside him the whole time just in case he tips over, even though Andrew thinks tipping over in Ball pose is a blast! He especially likes to tip and splash over into water that's only two or three inches deep. However, if you have a toddler who likes to play it safe, you can always place one hand on her midback to keep her balanced upright in the pose.

♡ Yogi Wogi Says

Yogi Wogi says, can you lift your feet and balance your ball on your bottom? When your preschooler is ready for a challenging treat, try Balancing Ball pose. Level II of Ball's Say n' Play shows you how. NOTE: Be ready to quickly put your hand behind your toddler so that she doesn't roll over backward as she learns how to lean back without falling.

⑥ Say n' Play: Level II

That's it, now ready ...   Sit in Ball pose while hugging below your knees.

lean back   Slowly begin to lean back.

lean back and lift your toes!   Lift your feet and toes a few inches off the floor. Continue to hug your legs.

That's it ... lift your toes!   If your toddler is hesitant, support her by placing one hand on her midback.

A balancing ball!   Cheer and be happy with your toddler!

Boat

Coordinated n' Confident Yoga

● ● ●

 Boat pose is a challenging pose that helps me be more confident, co-ordinated, and balanced. Younger toddlers might want to stick with Ball pose for a bit before trying Boat or begin with Boat's On the Go with Helen before moving onto the Say n' Play.

☺ Watch Me

1. Come into the preceding pose, Ball (page 153).
2. Extend your arms and hold the back of your thighs.
3. Lean back and balance on your bottom as you extend your legs one at a time.
4. With your hands holding the back of your thighs, extend both legs long and high.
5. Look at your toes and lift your head and feet upward.

6. NOTE: When your child is first entering Boat pose, please place one palm two inches behind (or on) your child's midback. This will give your toddler the support and balancing assistance he needs when beginning Boat pose.

⑥ Say n' Play

Come into Ball pose.	Have your toddler join you in Ball pose.
Arms long,	Extend your arms as you hold the back of your thighs. Your chest no longer touches the thighs as in Ball pose.
Arms long and	Encourage your toddler to extend her arms like you.
reach one foot up to the sky.	You and your toddler can begin to lean back slightly as you lift one leg up high.
Reach foot up to the sky! Good!	Place one hand behind your toddler and assist as needed.
Reach other foot up, up, high!	Show your toddler how to lift the other leg and foot up high!
Straighten your legs!	With your hands behind your thighs, fully extend your legs long and high.
Look at your toes!	Encourage your toddler to look at her toes and also float her head up tall on an inhalation.
Nice Boat pose!	Cheer your toddler on!

On the Go with Helen

After Boat pose, I treat my son to my rendition of "Row, Row, Row Your Boat." I reposition myself in front of him on the floor. Then we hold each other's hands as we lean back and forth and sing:

Row, row, row with me
Gently up the stream
Verily you're the cutest kid (or *girl* or *boy*)
I have ever seen!

♡ Yogi Wogi Says

Yogi Wogi says, can you sit tall in Boat pose and balance a Beanie Baby on your head? Try it and see!

✵ Whale ✵

Coordinated n' Confident Yoga

● ● ●

 Whale pose builds my coordination by introducing me to a new movement pattern. In Whale pose, I embrace a cross-lateral movement that I cannot see myself do—I can only feel its calming effect. Whales are considered big and intelligent sea creatures, and with this pose I will grow big and intelligent too!

☼ Watch Me

1. Encourage your toddler to lie on her tummy.
2. Lie on your belly. You may want to position yourself diagonally in front of your toddler to give her the best view of your feet when she crisscrosses in Whale.
3. Your forearms can support your chest as your head lifts upward.
4. Begin Whale's Say n' Play and invite your toddler to join you in the pose.

⑥ Say n' Play

Let's do Whale pose!	Lift your heels halfway to your tush.
Whale	Swing your heels sideways in a crisscross fashion.
pose.	Alternate which heel is in front and crisscross inward.
Whale	Swing your heels sideways in a crisscross fashion.
pose.	Alternate which heel is in front and crisscross inward.
Whale	Swing your heels sideways in a crisscross fashion.
pose.	Alternate which heel is in front and crisscross inward.

Repeat for as long as desired.

On the Go with Helen

When I introduced Whale pose to my toddler, I helped him feel the movement pattern of the pose by gently guiding his feet through its unseen crossing pattern. So, if your toddler hasn't begun to crisscross his heels yet or isn't alternating which heel comes forward, you can gently hold his shins and guide his feet through Whale's movement pattern. Come back down on your belly and try Whale again—you'll probably notice that your toddler's Whale pose has improved.

♡ Yogi Wogi Says

Yogi Wogi says, find your whale's spout. Can you make a whale sound? Show your toddler how to bring her lower lip out farther than the top lip. Exhale through your mouth, similar to how a whale lets steam out its spout. Psshhh! What else can your toddler do like a whale?

Bow

Coordinated n' Confident Yoga

• • •

 Bow pose is a fun stretch for growing bodies. It's positioning gently massages my internal organs. I used to think that Bow pose was difficult, but if I do Whale pose first, Bow pose is easy as can be! All I need to do is catch my feet and I'm in the Bow pose!

☼ Watch Me

1. From Whale pose, lower your chest and chin to the floor.
2. As you look forward, sweep your hands down next to your waist, one at a time.
3. Crisscross your legs as in Whale pose (page 159) once or twice to warm up for Bow pose.
4. Now catch your feet with the closest hand, one at a time.
5. Keep your chest low to the ground and your chin pointing forward.

Ready, Bow pose.	Come into the start position detailed in Watch Me.
Catch your foot.	Encourage your toddler to catch one foot. If she's having trouble, gently help her catch her first foot.
Catch the (other) foot.	As you continue to hold the first caught foot, catch the other foot. Or help your toddler catch her other foot.
Bow pose.	Rest on your bellies. Hands are holding ankles. Chins are on the floor.
Bow pose.	Continue to surrender into the stretch of Bow pose.

Repeat one to three times.

Finish with Child pose (page 43)

NOTE: During the toddler version of Bow pose, keep the feet close to the buttocks at all times.

On the Go with Helen

I like to share Bow pose with my toddler when he's tired but not interested in sleeping. Once in Bow pose, we close our eyes and rest for durations that successively increase in length. After a few Bow poses and perhaps part of the Blissful Bedtime routine, your child will successfully go to bed for a sound night's sleep.

♡ Yogi Wogi Says

Yogi Wogi says, let's use a dristi, or focal point, to keep your head looking forward in Bow pose. Place a small toy or stuffed animal eight to twelve inches in front of your toddler's nose in Bow pose. Ask your toddler to keep his gaze on the toy as he does the pose.

The Itsy Bitsy Coordinated n' Confident Yoga Routine

"I Can" Rap
page 147

Stack n' Clap
page 150

Ball
page 153

Boat
page 156

Whale
page 159

Bow
page 161

chapter 11
Quiet Time Yoga

● ● ●

Itsy Bitsy Yoga's Quiet Time Yoga is the perfect activity for your toddler before a nap or at the beginning of your preschooler's quiet time. The Quiet Time Yoga routine starts energetically and gradually eases your child into a calm, serene state:

- During the first pose, Buzzing Bee, your toddler has an opportunity to burn off any excess energy.

- In and Out helps toddlers learn how to consciously combine breath and movement.
- My Planet is a full body pose that helps your toddler become more aware of her surroundings and self.
- The last four poses of the Quiet Time Yoga routine are practiced on the floor or possibly in your toddler's bed: The side-lying Al-li-gator pose brings giggles into the day. Bridge pose strengthens and soothes the body. Legs Up is a restorative, yet playful pose. Lastly, Om-az-ing! boosts your toddler's self-esteem and cultivates calmness.

Throughout the routine, Little Spirita will continue to share each pose's specific benefits with you!

Buzzing Bee

Quiet Time Yoga

Buzzing Bee gets me buzzing with happiness! This pose helps me boost my coordination and motor-planning skills. It's a great way to add some structured exercise into my day.

Watch Me

1. Stand tall. Make two loose fists and place them close to the front of your shoulders. Your thumbs should be closest to your body.
2. As you breath mindfully, circle your elbows round and round. Think shoulder rolls.
3. Begin to walk around the room as you buzz! Wow, you've transformed from super Mom to buzzing bee! Now, let's get your little one involved by continuing with the Say n' Play.

Buzz, buzz, buzz.	Establish eye contact with your toddler as you continuously circle your elbows.
You do.	Encourage your toddler to do the pose by showing her how fun it is!
Buzz, buzz, buzz	Walk or jog around the room with your toddler following you!
buzz, Buzzing Bee!	Continue.
Buzz, buzz, buzz	Continue.
buzz, Buzzing Bee!	Continue.
Stop, other way!	Turn around to face the other direction. Reverse the circling of your elbows.
Go! Buzz, buzz, buzz	Walk or jog as you circle your elbows in the reverse direction with your toddler following you.
buzz, Buzzing Bee!	Continue.
Buzz, buzz, buzz,	Continue.
buzz, Buzzing Bee!	Continue.

On the Go with Helen

You can do Buzzing Bee to entice your child to follow you when she's more interested in staying put. You can practice Buzzing Bee in any kid-friendly environment. For example, if you're ready to leave the playground and your toddler isn't, let Buzzing Bee lead your child right to the car.

♡ Yogi Wogi Says

Yogi Wogi says, let's challenge our coordination! Try walking backwards while buzzing your bee wings (elbows and shoulders) forward.

Before you get started, make sure the space is clear. Please prevent your toddler from bumping into anything while walking backwards. This challenge is best suited for older toddlers who are ready to build new neuromuscular patterns.

In and Out

Quiet Time Yoga

• • •

 In and Out does more than just calm me; it improves my ability to walk backwards. During the pose, I also have an opportunity to explore moving through space in a directed fashion.

☼ Watch Me

1. Stand across from your toddler and hold her hands.
2. As you say the word "in," walk toward your toddler.
3. As you say the word "and," pause in place with your toddler.
4. As you say the word "out," both of you walk backwards to the start position. Continue to hold hands throughout In and Out.

⑥ Say n' Play

In	Hold hands and walk towards each other.
and	Pause with your hands down at your sides.
out	Walk backwards as far as you can while still holding hands with your toddler.

In	Now incorporate mindful breathing. Inhale as you walk towards each other.
and	Suspend (or hold the inhale) with your hands remaining down by your sides.
out	Exhale completely as you walk backwards to the start position.

Repeat five to fifteen times.

On the Go with Helen

During In and Out, you can match your toddler's energy level and gradually shift her into a calmer state. So, when your toddler is full of energy, begin by jogging "in" towards each other instead of walking. The "and" is a calm pause and the "out" can have the energy of a backwards jog. In subsequent repetitions, slow the pace to help your toddler wind down. Use the tone of your voice to reflect your child's excitement or to induce calmness.

♡ Yogi Wogi Says

Yogi Wogi says, try In and Out with all your family and friends! It can create a sense of oneness and get everyone working as a team. The more people participating in the pose, the merrier!

My Planet

Quiet Time Yoga

● ● ●

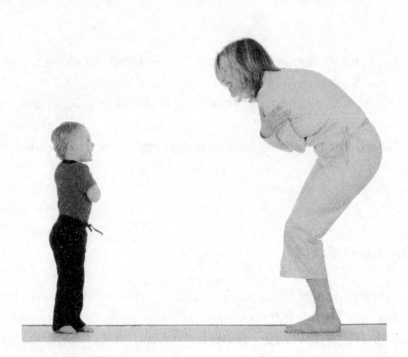

 When one of my two-year-old friends was getting dressed, he referred to his bottom as his basement. How creative and precious that he thinks his body is set up like his home! During My Planet, think of your body as planet Earth. We are one.

☀ Watch Me

1. Stand two to three feet in front of your toddler and establish good eye contact.
2. Show your toddler My Planet once or twice so she can become familiar with the pose.

⑥ Say n' Play

North Pole	Touch your head with both hands.
South Pole	Bend your knees and squat down. Touch your feet with both hands.
East Coast	Return to a standing position and open your left arm out to the side.
West.	Open your right arm out to the side.
Inside	Bring both hands to your chest.
outside	Open both hands out to the sides.
kiddo, you're the best!	Hug yourself and wiggle from side to side.

On the Go with Helen

Use My Planet to help a sometimes reluctant toddler get dressed. Say, "North Pole" as her shirt comes over her head. "South Pole" as you pull the shirt down. "East Coast" as the left arm goes into the left sleeve. And "West," as you guide her right hand through the right sleeve. After doing this, my son was no longer refusing to get dressed and was ready to continue with My Planet's Say n' Play.

♡ Yogi Wogi Says

Yogi Wogi says, practice My Planet on your favorite doll or stuffed animal. It's easy! Lay your doll in front of you on the floor. Now you can use your hands to guide your dolly into My Planet's Say n' Play.

Al-li-gator

Quiet Time Yoga

• • •

 All the mommies I know love Al-li-gator pose because it tones their outer thighs. I love the pose because it teaches me about balance and strengthens my legs!

☼ Watch Me

1. Lay down on your side with your legs extended and stacked.
2. For added comfort, place your arm under your ear.
3. Demonstrate Al-li-gator's Say n' Play for your toddler and encourage him to join you in the pose as soon as he's ready!

◐ Say n' Play

Al-   Lift your top leg up.
li-   Hold the leg up.
gator!   Briskly drop the leg down.

Al-	Lift your top leg up.
li-	Hold the leg up.
gator!	Briskly drop the leg down.

Crunch.	Flex your feet.
Crunch.	Extend and point the toes.
Crunch.	Flex your feet.

Repeat one to four times and vary the pace. You can either slow the pace for a calming effect, or speed it up for an energizing effect!

When ready, switch sides and repeat.

On the Go with Helen

 My son and I do Al-li-gator before bedtime. Typically we start with a faster paced pose and gradually slow down so we're ready for a good night's rest. Al-li-gator is a great way to get in one last bit of bonding before bed!

♡ Yogi Wogi Says

Yogi Wogi says, lie on your side and do a Double Al-li-gator. To begin, both you and your toddler lay in one long line facing the same side of the room. Moms, you have to bend the knee of your bottom leg so that your toddler's top foot can reach and press against your top foot. Now that you and your toddler are connected for Double Al-li-gator return to the Say n' Play for lots of fun!

Bridge

Quiet Time Yoga

● ● ●

 Bridge pose makes me feel strong, but I may need you to do the pose first so I can see what it's all about. My toddler friends love to say, "Ready, set, blast up" in Bridge pose with you!

☼ Watch Me

1. Encourage your toddler to lie down beside you.
2. Your hands can remain down by your sides throughout this pose.
3. Your toddler's upper back and shoulders should remain on the floor during Bridge pose.
4. Have your child watch you for the Say n' Play to learn how to blast up in Bridge pose.

⑤ Say n' Play

Ready ... feet near bottom!	Move your feet until your heels are about four inches from your bottom.
Set ... knees up!	Keep your feet on the floor as you bend both knees and point them up.
Blast up!	Lift your bottom away from the floor. Your shoulders remain flat on the floor.
Bridge pose, Bridge pose.	Your toddler can keep his bottom up in Bridge pose for five to thirty seconds (or as long as he'd like).

Repeat once or twice.

On the Go with Helen

 When my son was a little younger, I'd invite him into Bridge pose when I changed his diaper. Bridge pose can help you swoop the dirty diaper away and replace it with a clean one.

♡ Yogi Wogi Says

Yogi Wogi says, after Bridge pose, can you give your legs a big hug? Show your toddler how good it feels to hug your legs towards your chest after Bridge pose. This makes a great counter-stretch to the pose.

Legs Up

Quiet Time Yoga

● ● ●

 The "Itsy Bitsy Toes" song is like another of my favorite songs, the "Itsy Bitsy Spider," but I use my toes and legs instead of my fingers and arms. If I can keep my legs up in Legs Up pose, I notice how nurturing and restorative this pose can be.

☀ Watch Me

1. For Legs Up pose, you'll need about four feet of empty wall space. If you're tight on space, practice the pose behind a closed bedroom or closet door.

2. Sit down with your left side positioned close to the wall.

3. Lower onto your back and stretch your legs up against the wall. Your body will form an L shape.

4. Hold the pose for your toddler to see and explain that you're in Legs Up pose.

5. Encourage your toddler to sit next to you, with her back resting on the floor, bottom against the wall and legs up the wall. Your toddler's knees may have a slight bend in them.

6. Now you and your toddler are ready to sing the "Itsy Bitsy Toes" song in the Say n' Play.

⑥ Say n' Play

The itsy bitsy toes,	Form the L shape of Legs Up pose.
crawled up the empty wall.	Crawl your toes up the wall.
We stretched our legs up tall	Reach your toes up, and keep your back on the floor.
now our legs can fall.	Open your knees to the sides, allowing your feet to press together.
Vroom!	Slide your feet down the wall.
Then the itsy bitsy toes	Float your knees inward and return your feet flat on the wall.
crawled up the wall again.	Crawl your toes up until you form the L shape.
This time they'll stay here	Hold the pose for twenty-five seconds to several minutes.
until we say, "The end"!	
The end!	Playfully slide your feet down the wall.

On the Go with Helen

 After Legs Up pose, read your toddler a book as you rest next to each other. This pose can even be done in a twin bed positioned against a wall.

♡ Yogi Wogi Says

Yogi Wogi says, take some deep belly breaths as you rest in Legs Up pose. It can be fun to watch our bellies get full on the inhale and empty on the exhale. Some families may find it sweet to place a hand on each other's tummy during Legs Up pose. This allows everyone to reap the benefits of touch as they witness belly breaths.

OM-az-ing!

Quiet Time Yoga

● ● ●

 In OM-az-ing!, you can state positive affirmations to me and other toddlers. These positive remarks will have a lifelong effect on my self-esteem and our relationship. Mom and Dad, I want you to know I think you're OM-az-ing too!

☼ Watch Me

1. Sit with your toddler in your lap or seated across from you.
2. Hold your hands out in front of you with palms facing up. Press your index finger and thumb together.
3. Continue on to the Say n' Play. Your toddler will join you when he's ready.

⑥ Say n' Play

I am   Slowly bring your thumb and index finger together.
Om-az-ing!   Hold for "Om" and "az" and release on the "ing."

Repeat three to twelve times. Be sure to encourage your toddler to join you.

On the Go with Helen

 Tell your child why he's so amazing by remarking on special achievements throughout the day. For example, when he's potty training, you may say something like, "Sam used the potty. Sam is OM-az-ing! Sam used the potty and mommy said that's OM-az-ing!"

♡ Yogi Wogi Says

Yogi Wogi says, try doing OM-az-ing! with stickers. You'll each need two stickers. Place one sticker on the pad of your index finger and the other on the pad of your thumb. Now show your toddler how to bring the stickered thumb and index finger together in the pose. As with most new activities, you may have to demo it several times before a younger toddler gets the hang of it. Give preschoolers four stickers so they can do the pose with both hands.

The Itsy Bitsy Quiet Time Yoga Routine

Buzzing Bee
page 167

In and Out
page 170

My Planet
page 172

Al-li-gator
page 174

Bridge
page 176

Legs Up
page 178

Om-az-ing!
page 181

chapter 12
Blissful Bedtime Yoga

• • •

Yoga is a fabulous way for you and your young child to wind down from the day's activities. *Itsy Bitsy Yoga*'s Blissful Bedtime Yoga routine can be practiced anytime up until the moment your child falls asleep. You can elect to share all six poses just before bed or space them throughout your toddler's evening activities. For instance, you can practice the first pose, Flying Hearts, while your toddler is in the bathtub.

In the Blissful Bedtime Yoga routine you will find six poses to induce tender, loving moments at the end of the day:

- Flying Hearts is a fantastic chest opener that also helps rinse shampoo out of your toddler's hair with ease.
- Kissy Knee and Lil' Yogi are super-sweet poses that aid in digestion and elimination. While helping your toddler put on her pajamas, take a yogic break and practice Kissy Knee.
- Once your toddler is ready for bed, share Sleepy Star on her bedroom floor. This pose is super-soothing.
- Let you toddler know that her interests and preferences truly matter in I Like ... !
- And just before your toddler closes her eyes, sing the "Special You" song so she knows just how special she is!

Incorporate the Blissful Bedtime Yoga poses into your evening rituals and create some special memories that you and your toddler can treasure years from now.

For additional ideas on how to relax with your toddler or preschooler at any time, please see "End with a Short and Sweet Relaxation Activity" on page 30.

Flying Hearts

Blissful Bedtime Yoga

● ● ●

 Flying Hearts is a chest opener and gives me a way to look up and see the brighter side of life. When adults practice Flying Hearts, it helps prepare them for meditation, so you know its effect on me and other toddlers is calming too!

☼ Watch Me

1. Sit sideways in front of your toddler. Bring the soles of your feet together as your knees bend open to make a diamond shape with your legs.
2. Place your hands about three inches diagonally behind your hips. Your fingertips should point away from you.
3. Lean back slightly and lift your chest upward. Your knees can press downward.
4. Lift your head up and let your heart sing! Feel the joy of this chest and hip opener as you do this Say n' Play with your toddler.

⑥ Say n' Play

Flying Hearts,	Encourage your toddler to make a diamond shape with his legs.
Flying Hearts.	Lean back slightly, pressing your fingertips onto the floor.
You try!	You can assist your toddler's hands into position if needed.
Flying Hearts,	Lift your nose, chin, and heart upward.
Flying Hearts.	Breathe and enjoy the pose for fifteen to thirty seconds.
Let your heart sing,	Continue.
and do its own thing!	Do something silly or sweet!

Repeat one to three times.

On the Go with Helen

When giving my toddler a bath, I use Flying Hearts pose to rinse the shampoo out of his hair. Ask your toddler to "Let her heart sing" so her head, nose, and heart lift upward, allowing you to rinse shampoo off the top and sides of her head. For "and do its own thing!" ask your toddler to lean all the way forward to help you rinse the shampoo off the back of her head with greater ease.

♡ Yogi Wogi Says

Yogi Wogi says, after Flying Hearts pose, hold your feet and lean forward to share Eskimo Kisses with your toddler. Sit directly across from your toddler in Flying Hearts with your hands holding your feet together. Place your nose about six to eight inches in front of your toddler's nose. Reach your noses forward and wiggle your heads side to side, giving each other Eskimo Kisses. You may also feel a nice opening of the hips too!

Kissy Knee

Blissful Bedtime Yoga

● ● ●

 Kissy Knee improves digestion and elimination, which may be helpful to address before I ease off into a good night's sleep! This pose also helps quiet my mind. You may notice that Kissy Knee can bring out my caring, cuddly side.

☼ Watch Me

1. Sit diagonally across from your toddler.
2. Stretch one leg long in front of you.
3. Rest your other foot against the inner thigh of the extended leg.
4. Show your toddler how you take a deep breath to elongate the spine.
5. As you exhale, bend forward from your hips and kiss your knee! (If you find this difficult, you can bend your knee so you don't have to bend as far.)
6. Add kissing sound effects to make this pose more engaging for your toddler.

One leg out, stretch one leg out.	While seated, encourage your toddler to stretch one leg out long.
Other foot here!	The other foot presses into the inner thigh of the extended leg.
Now let's	As you inhale, sit tall.
Kissy Knee	As you exhale, bend forward to reach your nose to your extended knee.
Mmm! Mmm!	Move your head side to side as you kiss your knee repeatedly.
You try	Pause and look up at your toddler.
Kiss, kiss. Kissy Knee!	Come back down and encourage your toddler to kiss her own knee. Use lots of kissing sound effects.
Mmm! Nice Kissy Knee!	Give your toddler the thumbs up!

Repeat one to three times before switching legs.

On the Go with Helen

Use stickers to encourage your child into a nice Kissy Knee stretch. Give your toddler two stickers and ask her to place them on her knees. Invite her to bend forward and kiss the stickered knee that is extended long!

♡ Yogi Wogi Says

Yogi Wogi says, reach farther and let your fingers touch your toes in Kissy Knee. To show your toddler how, stretch your arms forward and see how close your fingers can come to your toes.

Lil' Yogi

Blissful Bedtime Yoga

● ● ●

In Lil' Yogi I get to do seated spinal twists! They make me feel so good because they help release tension. I'll twist to the tune of "I'm a Little Teapot" during the "Lil' Yogi" song.

☼ Watch Me

1. Sit across from your toddler with your legs out long. By sitting across from your toddler in Lil' Yogi your toddler gets to see you each time he twists back to the center.
2. Before you begin the Say n' Play, encourage your toddler to stretch his legs out long too.

⑥ Say n' Play

I'm a	With your legs out long, twist to the left.
lil'	Reach the fingertips of your left hand to the floor.
yogi	Turn your head to look behind you.
sweet	Rest into the twist.
n' smart.	Twist back to the center.

See me	With legs out long, twist to the right.
twist	Reach the fingertips of your right hand to the floor.
my	Turn your head to look behind you.
body	Rest into the twist.
n' heart!	Twist back to center.

Repeat three to five times.

On the Go with Helen

Whenever your toddler is shaking his head "no," transform the moment by introducing Lil' Yogi. It helps toddlers know how sweet they are while diffusing any frustration.

♡ Yogi Wogi Says

Yogi Wogi says, sit in "crisscross applesauce" and do Lil' Yogi. Twisting with your legs crossed offers a deeper stretch. As you twist to the left, bring the right hand to the left knee. When you twist to the right, your left hand rests on your right knee.

Sleepy Star

Blissful Bedtime Yoga

• • •

 The rocking motion of Sleepy Star soothes me into a good night's sleep! It also gives you and me a new way to connect after a busy day.

☼ Watch Me

1. While sitting, extend your legs out to the sides in an open V, and ask your toddler to do the same.
2. Bring your feet to your toddler's feet, creating a diamond shape.
3. With arms extended, sway your shoulders from side to side. Your torso will bend slightly to the side, allowing your palms or finger-tips to touch the floor in an alternating fashion during the "Sleepy Star" song I wrote for the Say n' Play.

⑥ Say n' Play

Twinkle,	Shift your shoulders to the right, with the right palm or fingertips coming to the floor.
twinkle	Shift your shoulders to the left, with the left palm or fingertips coming to the floor.
Sleepy	Shift your shoulders to the right, with the right palm or fingertips coming to the floor.
Star	Shift your shoulders to the left, with the left palm or fingertips coming to the floor.

Now that you have found the proper pace, continue this alternating motion four times for each line you sing.

You fill my day with lots-o-play.	Continue shifting right, left, right, left.
Now it's time to rest night, night.	Continue.
Go off to sleep without a fight.	Continue.

Twinkle, twinkle Sleepy Star	Continue.
I love everything that you are.	Continue.
Now it's time to rest night, night.	Continue.
Go off to sleep without a fight.	Continue.

Whisper the next two lines as you continue with Sleepy Star's movement.

Close your eyes and go to sleep.	Continue.
Let's lie down and not make a peep!	Continue.

Ask your toddler to lie down in his crib or bed. Use a soft whisper to sing the last verse to your toddler without any movement.

Close your eyes and go to sleep.
Let's lie down and not make a peep!
Twinkle, twinkle Sleepy Star
I love everything that you are!

On the Go with Helen

 I incorporate Sleepy Star into my toddler's bedtime routine. It's now a favorite good-night ritual, and even Daddy shares the pose with Andrew before bed.

♡ Yogi Wogi Says

Yogi Wogi says, can your toddler sing the words to the "Sleepy Star" song with you? Nothing is sweeter than hearing toddlers sing!

❋ I Like … ! ❋

Blissful Bedtime Yoga

● ● ●

The movement of I Like … ! helps me find calmness and focus whenever I am nervous or overstimulated. The pose also helps me communicate with you. In I Like … !, you'll learn what my favorite things are.

☀ Watch Me

1. Sit across from your toddler.
2. Ask your toddler any one of the following questions: "What animal do you like?" "What color do you like?" "What do you like to eat?" "Who do you like?" "What letter of the alphabet do you like?"

3. If you want, ask your toddler any simple question that would have a one-word response.
4. Follow the Say n' Play to learn the calming movements of I Like ... !

⑥ Say n' Play

I	Bring both fists to your heart (photo on page 197).
like	Open your arms out to the sides (below left).
(toddler's answer)	Bring your arms in and hug yourself as you wiggle side to side (below right).

Repeat with the initial answer three times.

The next time you practice the pose, choose a different question to ask your toddler.

On the Go with Helen

When driving with your toddler, transform I Like ... ! into I See ... ! When we are on long car rides or stuck in traffic, the whole family finds I See ... ! an enjoyable pastime. At first, older siblings or grown-ups can make the suggestions using what they see outside the window. For instance, "I see trees!" "I see trucks!" Then give your toddler the opportunity to tell you what she sees outside the car window. Backseat passengers can also do the associated movements of I Like ... ! pose.

♡ Yogi Wogi Says

Yogi Wogi says, choose one person, place, thing, event, or activity to appreciate and be thankful for as part of tonight's Blissful Bedtime routine. Ask your toddler, "What do you like today?" (You may need to repeat the question or give hints.) "Oh, you like Itsy Bitsy Yoga!" (Repeat their answer back to them.) "Let's do I Like Itsy Bitsy Yoga!" (Incorporate the movement found in this pose's Say n' Play.) This will build a solid foundation of compassion and gratitude in your young child.

Special You

Blissful Bedtime Yoga

● ● ●

The "Special You" song is full of affirmations that make me feel really special about who I am. It also playfully boosts my body awareness from head to toe!

☀ Watch Me

1. Sit or stand across from your toddler.
2. The "Special You" song is sung to the beat of "If You're Happy and You Know It."
3. As you move through the Say n' Play, place your hands to your own body parts and encourage your toddler to mimic you.

⑥ Say n' Play

If you're special and you know it, touch your head! Head!	Touch the top of your head.
If you're special and you know it, touch your eyes! Eyes!	Touch your temples.
If you're special and you know it, touch your throat! Throat!	Touch your throat lightly.
If you're special and you know it, touch your heart! Heart!	Touch your heart.
If you're special and you know it, touch your tummy! Tummy!	Touch your tummy.
If you're special and you know it, touch your belly button! Belly button!	Touch your belly button.
If you're special and you know it, touch your legs! Legs!	Touch your thighs.
If you're special and you know it, touch your feet! Feet!	Touch your feet.
You're special and you know it 'cause your body is here to show it!	Rub your hands together.
You are special and you know it— namaste!	Give yourself a soft, hug-like massage down your arms and legs.

Place your hands in the prayer position and bow to each other.

On the Go with Helen

I like to lie down and surrender completely to my toddler for the "Special You" song. Occasionally, Andrew brings his hands to his mommy's body parts during the song. So it becomes, "If you're special and you know it touch mommy's tummy! Tummy!" I still have to sing but I can sneak a little rest in while empowering him and receiving lots of love! This is a great way for exhausted moms to get a little afternoon rest.

♡ Yogi Wogi Says

Yogi Wogi says, try the "Special You" song on your favorite doll or stuffed animal. Ask your toddler to choose two dolls (or stuffed animals). If your toddler likes to be in charge, ask her which one you should use, and let her have the other one. Do the Say n' Play and place your hands on the doll's head, eyes, throat, and so on. Switch toys with your toddler and repeat. By switching, you're teaching your toddler to practice the yogic principle of nonattachment. And you're also promoting good sharing skills!

The Itsy Bitsy Blissful Bedtime Yoga Routine

Flying Hearts
page 187

Kissy Knee
page 190

Lil' Yogi
page 192

Sleepy Star
page 194

I Like … !
page 197

Special You
page 200

Acknowledgments

● ● ●

Katie McHugh, my editor at Da Capo Lifelong Books, for her vision and guidance. I'd also like to thank Wendie Carr and Lindsey Triebel, also at Da Capo, and Christine Marra for expertise in the book's finishing touches.

Natasha Kern, my literary agent, who is as passionate about books as I am about yoga!

Julie Carson May, for her dedication and uplifting presence!

Jill Recchia, Kristie Babbin, and Rachael Berkowitz, who helped make possible the beautiful images captured by the photographer, Tracy Bennett Stewart.

To all the lovely young children and parents who can be found enjoying yoga in the photographs in this book.

And, lastly, to all the Certified Itsy Bitsy Yoga Facilitators who teach weekly Baby, Tot, and Tyke Itsy Bitsy Yoga classes in at least twelve countries.

Super-Duper Yoga

• • •

The Itsy Bitsy Super-Duper Yoga Routine

Run around Yogi
page 73

Ring around the Yogi
page 135

Down Dog
page 45

Gorilla
page 118

I Like ... !
page 197

Yogi Yogi Feet
page 104

Tree
page 60

Buzzing Bee
page 167

Cobra
page 82

Whale
page 159

Burrito
page 87

Index

Resources

• • •

Visit ItsyBitsyYoga.com

- To download FREE Goodies
- To read Helen's Blog

Discover our Products—including DVDs, books, organic bamboo yoga clothing for babies and toddlers, Itsy Bitsy Yoga Mats, accessories, and so much more.

- Locate an Itsy Bitsy Yoga Class near you with our Class Locator
- Become a Certified Itsy Bitsy Yoga Facilitator